REINVENTED

REINVENTED

BERNICE SCHAEFER

ARPress

ILLUMINATING IDEAS.
EMPOWERING VOICES

ARPress
45 Dan Road Suite 5
Canton MA 02021

Hotline: 1(800) 220-7660
Fax: 1(855) 752-6001

Ordering Information:
Quantity sales. Special discounts are available on quantity purchases by corporations, associations, and others. For details, contact the publisher at the address above.

Printed in the United States of America.

ISBN-13:	Paperback	979-8-89389-089-1
	eBook	979-8-89356-789-2

Library of Congress Control Number: 2024909328

Table of Contents

Overview

Bernice Schaefer's memoir is a story of her journey from a 16-year-old girl to a respected psychologist and marriage and family therapist. Her story takes readers through the New York City of her childhood and teenage years as a star-struck celebrity "groupie." She marries and reluctantly moves to Connecticut where she single-mindedly educates and trains herself in several disciplines including opening and running a drama school, becoming trained as a psychodrama director and eventually becoming a counseling psychologist. Bernice became a Clinical Member of the American Association for Marriage and Family Therapy, a professional association representing over 50,000 marriage and family therapists throughout the United States and abroad.

We see her frailties, uncertainties, and vulnerabilities. She falls in love and marries shy of 19 to a man eight years her senior. Her husband dies at 66 forcing her to navigate a different life than that of her suburban enclave. She finds love again, but, that too, ends tragically. She learns that relationships bring with them the risk of abandonment. Relationships change.

Bernice Schaefer needed to adapt to that change as she matured. Her power, strengths, and internal resources enable her to develop independence. She feels that life is a continuation of elementary school, and we never lose that 10-year-old child within us. As we become more self-sufficient, we learn to love and support ourselves, comfort that child, and soothe the hurts that have been with us since childhood. Schaefer reminds us to trust ourselves, and if we have a goal, a vision, or an objective, know that the only way to reach it is if we permit it. Don't let anyone shatter your confidence.

Introduction

This "pearl of wisdom" is derived from my need to leave some tales about my life as a legacy for my family. It has become my story for anyone who may venture to read it with the assumption that some folks out there either share my spirit or will identify with a time in my life.

Many of my contemporaries talk about leaving special recipes to their children; I can plan a good menu, but my children and grandchildren cook far better than I do. I could give them a few lectures, but as far as life's lessons, I think they would do better to learn from their own mistakes.

My hope in writing this memoir is to give my readers a view of my past without a rose-colored filter, neither an accumulation of nostalgic melancholy, nor a glimpse of my life as pure pleasure and gratification, but a down-to-earth picture of my life as it was.

Acknowledgements

I'm most grateful to these people for the love and support they have given to me over the years.

Many of the people on this list are not in this memoir.

- My beautiful and caring daughter Janet who is never critical.
- Michael, my son-in-law, for being my financial adviser and friend.
- My oldest granddaughter, Emily, for her wit and wisdom, and for keeping me in her loop.
- Zoe, my granddaughter, who always has a good time and makes the best of all situations.
- My daughter, Rachel, equally beautiful, inside and outside, and for being there for me, always.
- Victor, my son-in-law, forever in my corner, and an amazing friend.
- Peg, my granddaughter, patient with any intellectual problem, every time a viable answer.

- Allan, my deceased husband, encouraging, an inspiration for his courage and balance.
- George, also deceased, my partner for fifteen years, accepting, approving, and supportive.
- Yuko, my youngest friend, for your thoughtfulness, and your technical and emotional guidance.
- Maria, my extraordinary friend and hairstylist, and to her wonderful husband, Jerome.
- Linda, my cousin, my good friend and confidant, now deceased and truly missed.
- Enid, my symbolic sister for your love and nourishment.
- Elaine and Ted, my oldest and devoted friends.
- Dee and Ed, wonderful playmates.
- Anita, my close friend of 69 years.
- For my special friends, both old and new, too many to list here, but you know who you are.
- Hank, my first writing instructor, and a motivating force.
- Carole, my friend, writing instructor, editor and trusted confidante.
- Jen, my friend and copy editor.

1

My Own Room

I know we're all told childhood memories aren't reliable until about three years of age – not true. I remember sitting on my mother's lap at nine months old. She wore a navy-blue bathrobe, her chestnut brown hair was long, and as she held me in her arms, she smiled down at my face with love and adoration. She wanted a girl after having two boys, and I was born a bright redhead, just like her dad. This was an image that I'll never forget, as I believe it was the only time my mother openly showed me that kind of love.

My grandparents were immigrants, my grandfather from Austria, and my grandmother from Hungary. They opened a clothing shop in New York City, not far from Central Park. They sold and tailored clothes for the very wealthy: the Rothschilds, the Lehman Brothers, even Vaudeville actors. They lived on the east side of New York City. Their business success allowed them to send their two daughters to college and one to nursing school.

Their only son, Mark, died at the age of 12 after being trampled by a horse in Central Park. My mother and her brother were very close, and I don't think she or her parents ever recovered from his death.

My mother's father died before I was born. His wife, my grandmother, died when I was 10. She was sick for years prior to her death, and my mother kept me away from her. Mom didn't want me exposed to serious illness. Her family didn't speak about cancer, it was the "C word."

Dad's father died before my brother Yale was born. Yale was nine years older than me. Four of my dad's six siblings also named their sons Yale. I was 12 when my grandmother died, a week before Yale got married. She was treasured by her children and grandchildren. She was warm and loving. We played cards together. I saw her once a year. She didn't speak a word of English, but was fluent in Russian and Yiddish. Her children could converse with her, but not her grandchildren. There were 14 cousins and I was the youngest.

At 21, my mother became engaged to a bright and interesting young man, but not good enough according to her parents, because he was a jockey. They pressured her into breaking her engagement off with Tom. I don't believe she ever forgave them for not accepting him. My mom played the piano, sang, and loved all the arts, especially opera. Tom supported her and enjoyed accompanying her to all events. Mom was devastated by the breakup.

When my mom was a young woman, Atlantic City

was where New Yorkers vacationed. She met my dad, Max, there while she was walking along the boardwalk with her sister. He was a tall and handsome, well attired man who was attracted by my mother's beauty. Their engagement was brief, and because he had his own business and seemed to fit my grandparents' idea of a successful husband, they married shortly after meeting.

My parents' marriage was stormy. I don't think there was ever real affection. They married for practical reasons. My mom was 24 and my dad was 31, older in that era for a couple wanting children. My mother's previous engagement was a real love affair, so it seemed her betrothal to my father was not colored by the adoration one hopes for in matrimony.

For my mom, it was a rebound relationship. For my dad, if Mom hadn't become pregnant on their honeymoon, he would have left the marriage. They had nothing in common. My mother liked the preforming arts and museums, while my father liked anything else. They were doomed from the start.

Although not a jockey like my mother's prior fiancé, my dad had a real love affair with horses, but more so with gambling. He played cards as often as he could and would bet on just about anything that seemed destined to win. I guess most gamblers think they won't lose. Dad never liked being passively seated, unless of course it was at a racetrack or a card table, so they only occasionally attended musical theater. They argued over just about everything, and their only commonality seemed to be the children. My mom eventually learned how to play cards just to endure social situations with Dad.

In the early 1930s after they married, my folks took an apartment in the Bronx since Mom wanted to live near her sisters. My two brothers were born in the five-room flat on the fourth floor off the Grand Concourse. Yale was born in 1929, Don was born in 1933, and I was born in 1938, which made Yale nine years older than me and Don four-and-a-half years older than me. My parents hired a nanny from Ireland to help with the chores and the children, and Sadie became part of the family.

After I was born, I slept in my parents' bedroom until I was four years old. Yale had his own room because my parents thought he was a genius. He needed his privacy and a quiet space to study. Don shared a bedroom with Sadie.

When I was about two, my informal acting career started when I learned to play dead. To exist in the same bedroom with my parents, I had to blend into the crib mattress and be completely silent. For two people who couldn't agree on what to have for dinner, they were lively and engaged in the bedroom. They, at least, had that in common.

But what were they thinking? Clearly my brothers should have shared a room. I should have slept in Sadie's room. My folks should have had their own room and the privacy that they needed.

When Sadie met a man at church and left us to marry before my fifth birthday, it seemed the bedroom arrangements would logically sort themselves out. As the only girl, I'd get my own room, and my brothers would finally share a room. Don was almost ten and old enough not to disturb Yale. Once again, my parents decided unwisely. They put me in Don's bedroom instead of having Don room with Yale.

Until then, Don and I had gotten along quite well. Once I moved into his bedroom, he declared war. We shared a closet, a desk, and a radio. We fought constantly. There was so little privacy in the house that the closet became my changing room. Don enjoyed coming into the bedroom while I was dressing in the closet and holding the door closed for what seemed like forever. I screamed while he laughed hysterically. No wonder why I suffered from claustrophobia for many years.

There was so much fighting at home that I found every reason to be elsewhere by the time I turned eight. My close girlfriend, Sheila, whose father was an executive at Columbia Pictures, was often left at home while her parents traveled. The maid supervised her while they were gone. Sheila's house became my second home. When her folks returned home on the weekends, they showed a movie on their eight-millimeter projector, usually a new one, on Friday nights. I was always included, as part of their family, and identified completely with all the redheaded movie stars that we watched in the films: Susan Haywood, Rita Hayworth, and Greer Garson. If the movie was too adult for us, Sheila and I hid under the dining room table and watched it anyhow. I'm certain her parents were aware, but they never said a word. After watching all those movies, I started acting, singing, and dancing around the house, convincing my parents to allow me to take lessons.

Although Dad never liked plays, he began to enjoy the plays I invented to entertain him. By the time I was nine, I learned to play a fierce game of gin rummy just to keep him company. I knew he was lonely. I realized at a young age that he had virtues and vices, and I loved him despite the contradictions. I believe my existence helped him find his inner spirit. He put me on a bicycle at three and never left my side while I rode. I was terrified but knew he would be there to catch me if I fell. He would walk with me for miles as I biked. He was my guardian angel. When he entered our house, I felt safe. I would look out of our window about ten minutes before he arrived home and I could recognize his walk for at least two city blocks. All he had to do was kiss me and tell me I looked beautiful, and likely added the single most important ingredient to my childhood. It gave me confidence. He was the only person I took "no" from, without question.

Just as I received the benefit of my father's warmth and love for me, I also believe most of my fears came from some of the decisions he made. As the secrets of human behavior are too important to be defined by a single episode, I think where I slept growing up – both with my parents and then with my brother – was certainly one of the issues that negatively affected my life. Claustrophobia took many years for me to overcome. Dad's anxious anticipation about the dangers of flying remained with me until my family wanted to visit new and distant places. I shared their curiosities about travel and didn't want to be left home. Boarding a plane, although difficult, became part of my lifestyle. Dad was averse to trying different foods and verbalized his dissatisfaction about how the foods influenced him. It wasn't easy, however, but I was determined to try everything new and exotic. Although fun to be with, Dad wasn't at all adventurous. I believe he paved the way for me to "know thyself." My quest was different. I was skeptical, but always moved toward conquering everything that frightened me.

My mother had a hard time with the attention Dad gave me and became even closer to and more enamored by my brothers. Mom was angry with me for just about everything I did or didn't do. Even if I wasn't hungry, I had to eat. If I finished my homework too quickly, she thought I didn't study hard. I'd climb out of bed in the morning and walk to the bathroom to brush my teeth; by the time I came back to the bedroom, my bed was made and mom was angry because I hadn't made it. Although she didn't like my father, the fact that he enjoyed being around me bothered her. My mother was not happy, and it was obvious. It made me sad. I, however, wouldn't allow my sadness to show, and that was when acting became an even bigger part of my life. In that regard, my parents were intelligent. They realized I needed something creative to keep me grounded. I started acting lessons with the Adler studio. The training was more professional than with Maria, my previous teacher. I would sometimes practice a scene at home during one of their arguments just to take the focus off my parents and put the attention on me. What they were fighting about was usually something trivial, but that was their pattern.

When I was 12 years old, Yale married his present wife, Betty, to avoid the draft during the Korean War. He was in law school. I loved Betty from the start, since she would be moving to another house with my brother, and I'd have my own room. Don moved into Yale's old room, and I finally had my private space. This new chapter in my life allowed me to read all the plays the library allowed me to borrow. I turned on the light during the night when I couldn't sleep and read until morning. Practicing scenes without a critic telling me what I needed to do was as important to me as dressing outside of a dark closet. That critic, of course, was my brother, Don. He began a program at The City College of New York to become an engineer, but he was also studying acting. We both appreciated the playwright, Tennessee Williams, especially passages from *Cat on a Hot Tin Roof*. I always liked the women Williams wrote about because they were often neurotic and very dramatic. We shared an interest in Williams but also liked John Steinbeck and Arthur Miller. I prepared scenes from many of their plays for my drama classes, and Don was familiar with all the sections that I chose. I couldn't hear anything constructive from my brother if we were living in the same room. We fought to survive. In separate bedrooms, we became amicable once again.

While I started life sleeping in my parent's bedroom, I now had a room I could call my own. Though difficult, the journey from one to the other led me to my greatest passion, acting. Now in my own room, I was free to express myself and to enlist my brother to help me practice. This was not only the beginning of my friendship with my brother Don, but it was also the beginning of my future in the theater.

2

Queenie

I'm nine years old. It's 5:45 p.m. and I run to the window. I open the blinds and look out onto the street, bustling with evening traffic, and wait to see Dad walking home from the subway station. As soon as he comes into view, I relax. I am always frightened this time of day when Mom is cooking dinner and her tension is evident. Although my mom is only 43, she appears older. Tonight, the frown on her face continues until dinner is over and the last dish is dried and placed in the cabinet. Her hair is severely tied up in a French twist; she looks hostile. Mom doesn't like the tedious chores of home-making. I secretly call her Mrs. Danvers, the evil housekeeper from one of my favorite books, *Rebecca*.

I'm worried about tonight. Dad arranged to get together with his brothers and Mom will be trapped entertaining her two sisters-in-law. I know she'd prefer spending time with her sisters and brothers-in-law. Dad's plans will incite harsh words from Mom.

We all sit down to dinner, promptly at 6:00. The kitchen, a small rectangular room, has a refrigerator, a four-burner stove, a sink, and a table that seats our family. My mother serves a four-course dinner every night. She grew up with that tradition. Mom's family had a cook and servants. What a life change for this woman. No wonder she's so unhappy. Dad makes a good living. He's in the garment industry, but likes cards and horses more than going to work, so money is limited. His employees don't like working hard either. My dad is convinced that most of his workers also play cards, instead of manufacturing dresses.

I don't like sitting at the dinner table. I always find something that I want to hear on the radio instead. If I say it's an assignment for school, I can often take my plate to the living room. I can't get away with this on a regular basis, but when I do, it's my chance to hide the food I don't want to eat. When I go to my best friend Sheila's house, I can consume what I want. I don't have to finish my dinner to get dessert.

We all sit too close to one another. I never have enough space. Don might break a tooth munching on a bone. Yale dominates the conversation. I choke down a few bites of food. Don kicks me under the table. I get angry. I automatically hit him. Mom yells at me. Even if I am the youngest, I should know better. Don sits there smirking and kicks me again. I kick him back. Fighting with Don takes my mind off the bickering between my parents.

Dad's presence soothes me. I am his "Queenie."

Pleasing Dad is my mantra. We take long walks. We play cards. Dad taught me the game of gin rummy. I often win. I must be competent, or he wouldn't want to play with me. I need to make him happy. That is my role in life. I never ask him for anything. Toys are almost non-existent. We get one present for Christmas and something practical for our birthdays. I make cut-out dolls from the cardboard that comes with Dad's laundered shirts. I glue shoe boxes together and stack them to make houses for my two-dimensional people. My parents always buy me new construction paper and crayons. I make a paste with flour and water. I create furniture, decorations, and clothing for the paper dolls. Dad is delighted by what I produce.

After dinner, Mom unties her long dark brown hair and lets it fall to her shoulders. With a softer face, she retires to the living room to sing and play the piano. Centered in front of the bay window, in the only formal living space in the apartment, is a small red-lacquered spinet piano. When she's singing or listening to music, Mom is beautiful. Her smile makes everyone in her presence grin from ear to ear. I try to avoid her until this time. I sit close by and listen to her perform. She might sing "Younger than Springtime" from the Broadway musical *South Pacific*, or she might choose the soprano solo of *Mozart's Mass* in C Minor. It's a "happening" to most people who visit our home. To us, it's what Mom does when she finishes her chores. Transformed into another world, a place exclusively hers, she generates magic with that remarkable instrument. There are always at least four or five neighbors listening at our apartment door each evening. They can't find better entertainment; hers is top-notch. If one of us leaves the apartment, neighbors greet us, "Hello." The people in our building stopped being embarrassed by their eavesdropping.

Mom sings opera but never became the professional she was trained to be. While she sings, I suspect she forgets that she cooks every evening for a man she no longer admires, and because of her bitterness toward him, I imagine that Dad has trouble caring for her.

After 16 years in our apartment, Mom wants to move. Our living quarters on the fourth floor of a six-story elevator building are cramped. There are three small bedrooms, one bathroom, a living room, and a kitchen. The apartment could fit into our summer bungalow. Years ago, my dad surprised us and bought a cottage in Long Beach. Dad's brothers have homes there, and they all play cards on the train, traveling to and from New York City each day. My mom wants to live there all year round and move from the city. She doesn't care that it's a summer community. She has privacy and space to move around, and the homeowner's clubhouse has a grand piano. Mom can play it anytime and is always asked to sing. The board of directors wants to pay her, but dad won't allow it. That creates another problem between my parents. We could use the additional money. Yale goes to college, and although clever enough to receive a scholarship, he needs books and clothes. I want to continue taking drama lessons, and Don needs a new lacrosse stick. I worry about our finances. What if we don't have the money to afford these things?

Playing cards and gambling on horses take extra money. Why won't Dad understand that and let Mom work? Mom is in a better mood tonight, now that she's had a chance to sing and play the piano. She walks me to my bedroom, tucks me in bed, and sings a few bars of James Lynam Molloy's "Love's Old Sweet Song." Dad comes in a few minutes later, kisses me, and says, "Goodnight, Queenie."

3

Born Last, Rarely Least

Although my family shared characteristics with many typical middle-class families during the 1940s and 1950s – educational aspirations, pursuing lucrative professions, joining cultural groups, and increasing social networks – there were a few notable differences.

My brothers Yale and Don were good students, the top of their classes. I was the youngest, the only girl, and not as studious as my older siblings, but bright enough to be able to enjoy the privilege of spreading myself as thin as possible in other fields. I was the artist, the dancer, and the attention getter.

I became my dad's favorite. Being the only girl was part of that, but I was also his enthusiast, conspirator, and supporter. Dad liked the fact that I watched him make smoke circles with his cigars and asked him to read his newspapers to me. When I saw him walking home from work, I waited and opened the door for him just before he was ready to enter the house. I appreciated his favorite radio programs and laughed with him in the right places. We listened to *Inner Sanctum, The Shadow,* and *Jack Benny.* He was an easy target. Not my mom. She thought I was a pain in the butt. She treasured my brothers and resented the fact that Dad thought I was sweet, funny and high-spirited. He never believed Mom when she told him I was spoiled, impudent, and impulsive.

I was the consummate actor who never needed scripts. I created them and performed at home, in plays at school, and wherever a child actor was needed so I could grab my share of attention.

Yale, the oldest, and Don, the middle, were musical. Yale played the piano by ear from age five. I gave the piano a short-lived run of about two years, but Yale's talent killed my passion. Don played the violin. We all giggled quietly for a long time until he caught the gist of that instrument and became commendable. He was persistent about everything he did.

I was people-oriented. I sensed what was vital at any given time and responded appropriately to move everyone into place. At four, I remember sitting on a blanket at the beach, where we had our summer bungalow. Yale stared at all the girls in their bathing suits, trying to muster up the courage to approach a young woman. I overheard him talking to his friend. I proceeded to walk over to several teenaged girls at different blankets, keeping in mind the one he wanted to meet, and asked, "Who would like to be introduced to my brother?" Yale was good-looking and aloof. His indifference made him more attractive. Several girls ardently said yes, and I proceeded to take them to the "king" in waiting. Finally, I marched over to the girl he admired most, took her by the hand, and brought her to Yale's blanket. She sat down with him, and they became fast friends. My brother, nine years my senior, who still calls me his kid sister, always tells that story. I did anything to achieve attention, but I also sought to make everyone happy.

Often, though, I was doing something mischievous. I was the child in the family who was chastised the most by my mother. If I wasn't sneaking out of the apartment, I was wearing my mother's clothes, her jewelry, or using her make-up. I never sat still.

Music was always a big part of our lives. If Yale wasn't at the keyboard playing Broadway tunes, my mom was heard singing while she cooked or sewed. Although trained in classical opera, she rarely performed outside of our home. If music was not live, the radio played in the background. We listened to opera, Beethoven, Mozart, show tunes, and movie scores. Different genres, but something to soothe our hearts. The house was never quiet.

My brothers were also athletes. They played stickball in the streets of New York City. When we went to the beach for the summer, they played baseball in a meadow at one of the neighborhood schools. Don enjoyed lacrosse in the 1950s, when they had wooden sticks with handles and three-foot long leather straps. The masks they wore protected their faces, but their bodies got badly battered. Don returned home looking like he'd been in an auto accident. My mother was afraid that playing lacrosse for The City College of New York would cost Don his life.

Both boys possessed the musical and athletic abilities I lacked, so it's no surprise I acted like a brat to get my share of attention. Last-borns are not taken seriously and forcefully must prove themselves. I became deeply conscious that I was the fledgling, the frailest, the feeblest, and the most dependent. As the youngster, I also accompanied my parents to more events than was customary or sensible for a child. I wanted to be important to my parents, so I rarely complained. It is no wonder that I am a psychologist. I needed to save my folks; they didn't like each other very much. My memories of childhood confirm that.

It was flu season, and I was five. We were all headed to see Dr. Brown for our inoculations. I was frightened by the thought of getting a needle in my arm. My dad told me that we would go for dessert afterward to my favorite ice cream parlor. That pacified me. Our handsome family doctor looked like Clark Gable and was soft-spoken and kind. I loved going to that office.

"Who will be the first one to get the shot?" Dr. Brown asked.

My father said, "Yale is the oldest, so the first needle will be in his arm."

Yale rolled up his shirt, saw the length of that pointer and fainted, knocking over the multi-tiered stainless-steel open cart that held all the doctor's bottles of medicine and the assortment of instruments used in his office. The mess was so bad that my mother started to cry. I became hysterical, and Dr. Brown softly said, "Oh, that long needle must have frightened Yale." I remember leaving the office and returning home, but don't remember ever going back for the flu shot. It was unforgettable for me. Going to the doctor was now a nightmare, I thought. It still is.

Shortly after that visit, my brother Don needed to have his tonsils out. You might think that my folks had one of our friends or relatives care for me so they could take my brother to the hospital by himself. Don was high-strung, although it only surfaced when he was frightened. He was nine, and verbal about not wanting to go the hospital. An unpleasant scene in the taxi made me wonder why I was along for the ride. What seemed like forever in the admitting office was followed by a trek to Don's hospital room. The nurse came in to put a dressing gown on my brother, and Don started climbing the walls. I had never witnessed anything quite like this, even in the movies. As angry as I could be with my brother, I started to cry; I was sad for him. He was frantic. Two years later when I was about to have my tonsils removed, I cried for two days before the surgery. I screeched as they put the mask on my face and asked me to count backward from 100.

Yale was in school, excused from these enduring (life-changing) experiences. These occasions became family outings. Observing my parents' choices about what was appropriate for their children, I'm sure Yale witnessed many disasters before my birth. I would imagine that the "flu shot" fiasco we had with Dr. Brown strengthened my parent's decision to let Yale stay in school that day.

I loved going to the movies. At nine, if I wanted to join my friends to see a Saturday movie, I was reminded that I had to plan on spending Sunday with my parents at another film. They wanted me as their shield, although I didn't realize that until I was older. My brothers could do what they preferred and often stayed home. It didn't matter what was playing; if it was a Sunday and we didn't have any obligations, the cinema was our church, the only one that sold candy. I was not a good eater and pounds lighter than girls my age. Mom insisted on bringing a sandwich to the theater. If I wanted candy, I had to eat what she brought with her. She knew that I had a ravenous sweet tooth and would eat her sandwich just to get my sweets.

One Sunday, *The Snake Pit* was playing, along with another equally terrifying film. I identified with the protagonist. Just as I was confused as to why my two outwardly normal parents always seated me between them, Olivia de Havilland was equally muddled as to why she found herself in a mental hospital with no memory of her entry there. This psychological drama plagued me for months. Virginia, the central character, was afflicted by delusions and mistreatment, by cruel nurses and disturbed patients. She was drenched by a hose, put in a straitjacket, and thrown into solitary confinement. I was as horrified watching this film as I was observing my brother climb the walls in the hospital while waiting to have his tonsils removed.

I could read my family from a young age and see what was required. I couldn't compete with a first-born megastar, or an athletic, obedient middle brother, but I was entertaining and funny. While I was temperamental, impatient, and self-centered, I was also thoughtful, obliging and loving to my parents. I gave them what they couldn't give each other.

Forever the youngest child, I still find myself playing the pleaser, the diplomat, the actor, and the sometimes-bewildered witness. My childhood role as the youngest of three was, and still is, a part of me that I can acknowledge, honor, use to my advantage as I move into the latter part of my life. It defined, and, perhaps more importantly, saved my life as a child. For that, I can truly be grateful.

4

Florida, Here I Come

In 1953, I went to Florida to visit my best friend Sheila and her family in the middle of winter. They owned a home a block from the ocean. Excited and counting the days, I kept my suitcase open and next to my bed for two weeks. I didn't want to forget anything.

Sheila visited me and my family at our Long Beach cottage for a few days. Her mom drove her to our place from the city. She was the only mother of anyone in our crowd who owned a car. Sheila lived in a penthouse a block from my apartment. Columbia Pictures promoted her dad to vice president, and that meant traveling to California several times a month. They had several maids to keep their place clean and to prepare the meals. I spent all my spare time at her house, imagining I was in Hollywood.

Gert, Sheila's mom, said to my mom, "We would love to have Bernice come to Florida with us during February vacation. She can fly down with our family and stay for two weeks. We usually have a house full during the second week, and it'll be fun. Our children will stay an extra week, but we would be happy to drive Bernice to the airport and wait with her until the plane takes off."

My mother looked shocked and said, "We don't fly. My husband travels for business but only goes by train, boat, or bus. He would never let Bernice take an airplane."

"What about the train?"

"I will have to talk to Bernice's dad. Thank you for the invitation," Mom said to Gert. "We'll discuss it and let you know."

My parents said it was costly, but I could go if I was willing to travel as a 12-year-old. Half-fare. With my January birthday, I'd be 13 a month before the trip.

"And you will have to sit up all night," Mom said. "Compartments on the train are expensive."

I wanted to go on this holiday any way that would get me there. We rarely travelled as a family. I was surprised they would consider letting me visit my friend so far from home – and by train! I had only taken the train once before, when we traveled to Vermont for a family vacation. It was a sleeper like in the movies. The dining car was remarkable. Women were dressed in evening gowns and some ladies wore hats. Candles, flowers, and silver decorated the tables. The subway cars I took to school each day couldn't be considered trains.

I couldn't take my old summer stuff to Florida. All Sheila's outfits were from Saks Fifth Avenue and the latest styles. I didn't care about what was stylish, but I wanted to look nice. I worked during the summer for Paul, a man who owned a store a few streets away from our summer cottage. Legally, he couldn't hire me. I was only 12. I talked him into letting me work for just one day.

"You won't have to pay me, just watch me fold garments and stack them. If you like what I do, you can let me come in a few days a week. I love kids, but I don't want to babysit again," I told him. "The work isn't steady."

His store had pretty things. He said they were "seconds," but they looked perfect to me.

Paul said, "You have a good attitude, and you're fast. I will pay you 50 cents an hour, in cash." I kept 25 cents each week for spending money and used the rest in his store. I bought shorts and skirts and bathing suits, as many things as I could afford to buy.

The day I left was a snowy Saturday morning. I was ready to go. I looked out the window and thought, *tomorrow I will be on the beach, swimming in the ocean.* It was hard to believe that life could be so different in just 24 hours. I hadn't slept. I was thrilled and frightened at the same time. We took a cab to Penn Station. I was quiet. Nobody spoke.

My mouth was dry, I couldn't swallow, and I had a hard time breathing. My stomach felt as if it was full and I hadn't eaten. My foot didn't want to take that first escalator step. My legs felt numb; I thought I was going to fall. My parents were in front of me. The noise was deafening. I wanted to turn around and run away.

The train was called *The Streamliner*. It was steel and

sleek. Draped over each seat was a plaid blanket. My parents waited until the train was ready to move and they were finally asked to leave. I watched them walk off the train and I started to cry. I was embarrassed. I ran to the bathroom. My hair, usually long and smooth, was in braids, and my mother tied a bow on each one. Black jeans, a white blouse, and white sneakers made me look younger than 13. I felt ridiculous. I locked the door, looked in the mirror and couldn't stop crying.

How could my parents let me look like this? How will they manage without me? Why did I leave them? I wanted to go home. Florida seemed too far away. I washed my face and decided to make the best of this ride and the trip. I tried to unlock the door, but the latch wouldn't budge. I was locked in the bathroom. I started pulling on the door; I couldn't get it to move. I called out, "Can anyone hear me? I'm locked in the bathroom." The train left the station. I sat down on the toilet seat and started to cry again. I waited a few minutes and pounded on the door.

After what seemed like an eternity, a man finally caught what I was saying. I was sobbing, "I can't open this door. I don't know what to do." He said he would be right back with someone who worked on the train. A short time later, a man with a very reassuring voice was at the other end of the door and said, "No one has ever been left in the bathroom. Please be calm. Jiggle the lock; it sometimes gets stuck."

I was frantic at that time. I kept moving the lever back and forth with no success. I finally got the door open. I was out of the lavatory, but I didn't feel free. I was disheveled and scared. The conductor was kind. He took me by the hand and brought me to the dining car. "Order anything you'd like; the meal is on us. Enjoy the rest of your journey."

5

The Seagull

Sheila was a weekly guest for dinner at our household. Those evenings were always pure pleasure for Don and me, since my parents, impressed with Sheila's lightheartedness, her spunk, and her parents' wealth, were on their best behavior. Sheila was a celebrity among our friends in the Bronx. Her parents had a ten-room penthouse apartment half a block from our house, and her world was different. Her mom and dad were never home during the week. My folks were always home. Gert, Sheila's mother, was in New York painting. She became an artist in her middle years, and a competent one. Sheila's Dad was, as we later found out, off with Gert's best friend who also had the name Gert. Sheila and I laughed about this coincidence in later years, as we realized that at a tender moment saying the word "Gert" would delight them both. We were amazed how he juggled his relationships with both Gerts for over 25 years. Sheila's sister was four years older, and most of her evenings were spent at her boyfriend's house. Most nights, if I wasn't her guest, Sheila would have dinner alone and could be lonely. Dinner at my house was a treat for her.

Our dinner was served promptly at 6:00. Dad arrived home at 5:55, washed his hands, then we sat down at the table. Mom prepared a hearty meal, one that corresponded with the day of the week, so everyone always knew what we were having for dinner. On days that we were having fish, I'd try to eat at Sheila's. If Mom changed the menu without telling my dad in advance, an argument began. My dad seemed to think that something dreadful would happen to him if he had meat twice in one day. Mom explained to dad that occasionally the fish market wouldn't have fresh flounder or grey sole, and because she couldn't reach him (no phones at the racetrack), she was forced to improvise.

Once seated, my brother Don inevitably spilled his glass of milk, because he anticipated the tension that existed between my parents during dinner. If it wasn't a menu change, my dad complained, "The meat is too rare, put it back," or "I had meat for lunch, I thought we were having fish." We all knew that dad left his office early to play cards or visit the racetrack, and he usually lost. On winning days, very rare occasions, he might say, "Hmm, this is good." When he finished complaining about the meal, he scolded Don for being so clumsy. I was confused, as I felt sorry for Don for being humiliated, but the milk usually spilled on my lap, so I was furious. I kept quiet.

It was the early 1950s and I was thirteen, exploring

the world of movies and theater. That was as exciting as spending a night alone with Sheila at her house, making phone calls to people, using my newly acquired British and Southern accents. Hours were spent speaking to strangers over the phone, using different dialects, telling them that they won prizes or trips to mysterious places. With Sheila's travels and her father's affiliation with the motion picture industry, it might be assumed that she came by all this playacting naturally. I was the instigator and she was the follower. Sheila went along with me just for fun. I was thrilled with my acting classes and all the new scenes I was preparing, and I often daydreamed about going to Hollywood or to some Arabian country. My parents took me to see *Kismet* at the Ziegfeld Theater as a present for my birthday. This experience only increased my desire to see more plays and travel someplace out of the ordinary. Sheila and I wanted to swap lives. She was blissful spending time telling my mom her most cherished secrets, and I was happy to stay with Sheila and her maid, Maud, looking at movie and travel magazines and practicing my scenes where there were no parents around to listen. Sheila and Maud made the perfect audience.

As much as I didn't enjoy babysitting, I took care of two children several evenings a week to earn enough money for tickets to plays and the silk blouses and fitted skirts to wear to them. We had to look grown-up to be part of the Broadway scene. My parents thought that tickets to shows and my taste in clothes were extravagant for a girl my age, and unquestionably only items I would receive as gifts. To me, they were necessities.

Don't get me wrong, I loved children, but these babysitting jobs, inherited from my brother, were horrible. Don was in college and no longer had the time. The two boys he cared for on separate nights were spoiled. They were antisocial, only children, with poor impulse-control. They missed my brother and took their frustration out on me. A moment or two after the parents left, a boulder was often thrown at my stomach, or I might be pushed and tripped, then tied up. I threatened to tell their parents so I could eventually be untied. I didn't want the parents to know about their behavior, as I feared they'd hire a boy to replace me. The money was good, and I needed the funds to support my lifestyle. I continued babysitting until I found a real job. I was lucky enough to find work the next summer at a clothing store. I was too young to be put on the payroll, but because I was a hard worker, I was paid in cash. I never baby- sat again, and I made enough money that summer to support my habits during the next year.

Sheila always had an abundance of spending money, and she knew she was more privileged than most of our friends. Her affluence brought out some unusual behaviors that our friends were fearful of doing. She shoplifted in Woolworth's by taking a large umbrella into the store and stealing small items that were easy to put in her closed umbrella. We stood guard, frightened. She stopped after a few times, and we missed the excitement, but were happy she never got caught. I was convinced that if I ever took a lipstick without paying, my parents would be called to pick me up from jail.

Sheila introduced me to "second acting" all the plays we saw on and off Broadway. We walked discreetly into the theaters during intermission, without paying for a ticket, to see the second act. We were both star-struck and adored Montgomery Clift. I saw him four times in the movie *A Place in the Sun*, and at least five times in *From Here to Eternity*. I was madly in love. I think Sheila went along with me because, again, my excitement was entertaining for her to watch. My drama teacher, who knew about my infatuation, told me that Montgomery Clift was starring in *The Seagull*. I had never been exposed to Chekhov's plays. We learned that Clift was opening at the Phoenix Theater, off Broadway, with Maureen Stapleton as one of his co-stars. We couldn't wait to take the subway to the city and buy tickets. When we arrived at the theater, we realized that the tickets were costly. We were willing to buy two tickets, despite the cost, but they were sold out. Extremely disappointed, we decided to wait at the stage door and at least get a glimpse of him when the play ended. At intermission, Sheila saw several people leaving the theatre and convinced me to walk in with her, and find two seats, preferably apart from one another. It worked. We found two seats within three rows of the stage and stayed for the second act. The play was wonderful! The acting was superb, and I was overjoyed. We waited at the stage door after the show and saw Clift. We watched him glide into a cab and without even thinking, we hailed the next one, saying, "Follow that cab."

The taxi drove to a brownstone on the west side of 65th Street. At first, we weren't sure if Clift lived there or was visiting someone. We later found out it was indeed his home. We must have followed him at least eight times. I think we found "follow that cab" just as exciting as the eight times we saw the second act of that play. We finally bought a ticket to see the complete performance. I was in awe of Chekhov's masterpiece.

After the second time we saw the second act of *The Seagull*, I borrowed the play from the library. I liked it so much that I bought a copy from Samuel French, who sold inexpensive editions of individual plays. I memorized most of the lines by the time I saw the full production. The setting was beautiful, the country estate in Russia was glorious, and the portrayal of the characters was so genuine. The devastated dreams and lost hopes of the brilliant cast reminded me of my family, especially my parents. The dying seagull represented the emptiness of defeat. It also emphasized the beauty to be found in life. Irena, the mother of Clift's character, reminded me of my mom; although in the play, Irena was a famous actress and a member of the artistic community. This would have been my mother's dream, to be a writer, a singer or a piano player. There was a good deal of envy in this play, not unlike what I saw between Mom and her sisters. My mother was the prettiest and brightest of the three women, but the most unfulfilled. My dad never wanted my mother to work. I was in high school when Mom finally got the courage to defy him by getting a job as a buyer at Arnold Constable, a department store in Manhattan. She would come home tired, but didn't worry about what was for dinner. She was somewhat content, finally.

The local schoolteacher in the play who wanted to be wealthy was just like my father, but not as dynamic. Dad's dream of being as prosperous as his oldest brother dominated his life. My uncle and dad worked in the same type of dress manufacturing business. The union told them both that they had to join or lose support and their business. My uncle joined the labor union and became very wealthy. My father, stubborn as he was, said, "They can't tell me what to do." Once again, my dad made a big mistake. He didn't join the union and they put him out of business. Luckily, my dad was quite comfortable up until that time. We lived on the money he saved for most of my childhood.

My brother embodied the part that Montgomery Clift portrayed. Engineering was not his forte. He completed college and worked as a civil engineer for about two months. He hated that kind of work. He was an artist, an actor and writer, and he struggled to find his voice. Like Konstantin (Clift's role), my brother and my parents were dreamers. I felt at home watching that play, as if sitting in my living room. There were loving moments, which we had as well.

Once the play left New York, Clift went to Hollywood to make a movie, and our loyalties shifted to Eddie Fisher. Sheila and I became veterans of second acting most of the plays in New York. Occasionally we bought a ticket, but our money had to be saved for taxi cabs. We started following Eddie Fisher to all his engagements. We were on his tail to his hotel, usually the Algonquin. We learned what floor he was on by watching where the elevator stopped. Then we walked the stairs to his floor. There were elevator men in the '50s, and two young ladies wouldn't be warmly received trying to ride up to bother a guest, particularly a famous person. We sometimes had to walk 20 flights of stairs, find a comfortable place to sit on the floor, and wait for him to leave his room.

We made that trek so often that Fisher got to know us by name. He'd say, "Hello Bernice, Hello Sheila," with a chuckle. These were the days when they often had stage shows after a movie in many New York theaters. Our excursion started at the stage door while we waited for Fisher to exit the theater. Occasionally we'd buy a ticket to see him, but the movie, before the stage show, was a strange version of *The House of Wax* with Vincent Price, and we disliked it immensely. Following Eddie Fisher by cab to his hotel and seeing him near was more exciting.

We'd be called stalkers if this happened today.

All the groupie stuff ended for me the following summer in Long Beach; I met my first real love. Four of us were crazy about Dave, a young man who came from Boston to stay with his dad for the summer. I was not one to chase him the way my friends did. I think I was boy shy at that point, although shy wouldn't have described me in most other ways. I kept my distance, and he ended up liking me and spending most of the summer at my bungalow. My friends at the beach were no longer my friends after that, and for a while it hurt. Eventually, it didn't really matter since those girls joined a beach club. I had to work. I spent an isolated summer without girlfriends, but I had my first experience with a boy who made up for my first involvement with mean girls. This crowd was very different from my friends in the Bronx.

6

Senior Year

Pamela and I walked down a familiar hill to my apartment, having just been out for pizza to celebrate the end of our school week. We commiserated about the shortage of grown-up boys in our senior class at Taft High School. Pamela spent the night at my house and joined me at drama school on Saturday. I rehearsed several scenes from Arthur Miller's *After the Fall* and Shakespeare's *Romeo and Juliet*, plays we studied for almost a year. Pamela was looking forward to sharing my excitement about the theater. At this stage of my life, drama and boys were my passions. With much enthusiasm, I confided to Pamela that I met a young man, Howard, a few weeks before at the Paradise Movie Theatre. He phoned me frequently. I got a little giddy describing Howard, a bright redhead with big freckles who looked so similar to me he could pass for my brother. In the past, any redheaded male who resembled me was the last person on my dating list. But Howard was nice and funny. At 16, I practiced the art of camouflaging my flaws with makeup, so I covered my freckles with Max Factor foundation, and in my mind, looked prettier. Howard could do nothing to mask his freckles.

After talking on the phone for weeks, I finally agreed to go out on a date with Howard, though I had a hard time envisioning us as a couple. The thing which most allured me was that he was 21, which made him infinitely more appealing than the younger boys in high school. I vowed to give Howard a chance and enjoy the evening. Howard asked me to bring along a friend to introduce to his friend, Roland. Pamela wasn't available that weekend, so I brought Sheila. Since I barely knew Howard, I was happy to double date with Sheila and Roland, who was quite charming, nice looking, and more mature in appearance and manner than Howard.

Sheila and Roland didn't hit it off. They couldn't find any common interest and barely spoke all evening. Howard seemed to enjoy my company, and I felt the need to be as interesting as possible, so I regaled Howard with stories about my fellow drama school students. Although I was attending the American Academy of Dramatic Arts part-time, I made it sound as if I were a full-time student.

I told them about Marybeth, my friend from drama school who had tattoos covering her arms, though it wasn't trendy at the time. She looked outlandish. Millie wore her hair short and in spikes. She was always acting on stage or off. Chuck had anger management issues. He often threw things at people when he felt that he ruined a scene.

Howard and Roland enjoyed these tales of my class-mates, but I was really still just a high school senior. After dinner, the four of us drove across the George Washington Bridge to a New Jersey nightclub. The drinking age was 18, so Sheila and I got all dressed up. I wore a powder blue fitted dress (bought for my role in *Our Town*) and three-inch heels. Between the outfit and the makeup, I easily passed for 18. Sheila did too.

Howard called the next day, looking for another date the following Friday. Once again, he asked if I could introduce Roland to another friend. My friend, Anne, and her boyfriend had split, so she was eager to date. Anne was petite and Roland wasn't too tall, so, at least visually, they seemed like they'd make a nice match. Another poor choice. They were completely incompatible. I was chatty again and grew bored with having to be an actress on my dates with Howard. I completely lost interest in Howard and decided not to date him again. He called the next day to ask me out, and I made excuses for that night and all the evenings after that. He was perceptive enough to get the message and didn't call back. Two days later, Roland called, and I was pleased to accept a date with him for the following week.

Roland came from a prestigious area of the Bronx called Riverdale. We spent many evenings after that dating. I can't recall what we did on our dates, but I remember attending nightclubs and movies. I remember the way he kissed, though. He was sensuous, and although I already had a steady beau a few years prior, I had never been kissed like Roland kissed me.

That Friday evening, walking down the hill with Pamela and telling her the story of a new boyfriend, we entered my apartment building and pressed the "4" button to go up to my unit. For some mysterious reason, the elevator took us down to the basement. It seemed strange, but we pressed "4" again, and this time, the elevator stopped at the main floor where a man was looking at us through the glass window motioning for us to come out. It surprised me that we weren't frightened. It was the 1950s, and from age 11, I took the subway to drama class in Manhattan by myself. Also, Sheila and I took the subway to Central Park to ice skate often. Consequently, two men in the lobby of my building didn't seem all that scary.

Pamela and I spent about an hour and a half talking to the two men, who revealed they followed us down the street to my building. They were not boys. Allan was very handsome. He was blonde, blue-eyed, and well-spoken. He was a second-year law student who lived in an apartment across the street. He was with his friend Hal, who was interested in Pamela. Allan and Hal just returned from Yonkers' Raceway and won a good deal of money. They suggested spending some of it on us the next night at a restaurant. Dominick's was a wonderful steak house and eventually became a place where Allan and I enjoyed many evenings together.

Again, what was I to do? If I told Allan I was a high school senior, he would have been amazed and likely scared off. Fearing he would think I was much too young, I decided that truth seemed too risky, so I told what I considered to be a little white lie.

Allan was bright, sophisticated and drove a cab part-time to supplement the trust fund left to him by his grandparents for his education. He was originally from West Hartford, Connecticut, and moved to New York where he eventually attended college and then New York University Law School. He didn't have a New York accent which was very appealing to me since my elocution teacher was working very hard to rid me of mine.

My time with Allan was a joyful period for me and he turned my life around. We loved the movies, Chinese food, walking and talking, or seeing Broadway plays. I no longer saw just the second act of all the plays I wanted to see in New York City. Thanks to Allan, I could attend a complete production whenever we had time. We usually dated once during the week and on weekends. I still liked Roland and saw him several nights throughout the week. I suspected he was dating someone else too, a woman as important to him as Allan was to me. From October until June, I dated two men without either of them discovering my secret. I didn't lie to Allan; he just assumed I was busy during the week when we weren't together, and I was. I had lots of homework and a busy social life, plus drama school. About three months into my relationship with Allan, I revealed I was a high school senior and a part-time drama student. I think he was in love by then, and although he was embarrassed to share this story with his family, he accepted my age and high school status. I was relieved.

From the beginning of June through Labor Day, my

family spent summers in our Long Island bungalow. We were one of the few families without a telephone. I had to make some decisions about how to balance my two boyfriends. Allan's love for me was very deep and very possessive. He wanted to spend weekends with my family and me at the beach, so I realized that things had to end with Roland. I wanted to, needed to, choose Allan. I told Roland I didn't have a phone and he said he'd write in a few days. He did. He also asked me to call him to plan an evening together during the following week. I didn't know what to say. I never replied.

7

Leaving Home

It was the late 1950s and I was preparing to graduate from high school. I asked Allan, the man I started dating in October, if he would escort me to my senior prom. He was in his second year of law school. I thought he might have some reservations about spending the evening with much younger adults.

Much to my surprise and delight, Allan said he would be happy to be my prom date.

I spent the afternoon shopping for a dress at Arnold Constable, a New York department store, with my mom, who at 5'4" could have modeled the ladies fashions that she purchased for the store. Mom started to work when I turned 15. Not only could my parents use the money, but my mother wanted her sanity. Preparing meals, reading, and dining with the ladies became boring and depressing for her.

Mom was artistic, had impeccable taste, and when she was content, was cheerful and optimistic. Working in retail was perfect for her. She first worked as a sales associate, developing a good rapport with customers who appreciated her honesty and made her a valued employee. A few months later, she became the purchaser for designer clothes, the store's first personal shopper.

Excited about taking me to work, Mom said, "You can buy anything you want." I found a beautiful aqua dress: strapless, tea length, with small seeded pearls sewn on the bodice. Sandals would be dyed to match.

Later that evening, Allan and I ate dinner at Dominick's, our favorite steak house, when he said, "I think I found the perfect piece of jewelry to go with your new dress. You can wear it now, or save it for the prom."

He took a large box out of a non-descript bag and handed it to me.

"I hope you like it. You can return it if it isn't what you want. I love you and would like you to marry me. How about a year from October?"

Inside the big package was a small ring box with a beautiful diamond – perfectly sized. I couldn't speak. Tears flooded my eyes, and I started to cry. Allan was handsome, kind, generous and smart, and I was madly in love. I was fortunate, and I knew it. At 17, I was the first of my friends to become engaged. Allan was 25 and would be graduating law school the following year.

We went to my house and shared the news with my parents. They were happy for us. After our third date, Allan became a beloved member of the family. He had an apartment across the street from our building and dined with us at least once a week. His disposition was very different from anyone in my household. My family was intense and dramatic. Allan was calm and relaxed.

Allan always had a twinkle in his big blue eyes. He looked upon life as an adventure. Allan said that his first year of law school was "busy work." The second year, once we started dating, he put his books away after a few hours, and said, "it's time for a walk and an interval to think about what I just read." His life was always balanced.

That evening, we set our wedding date. It was October 21st, two years minus a day from when we first met. My folks wanted to know what kind of celebration we might consider. They suggested a small party so there would be enough money available for us to buy furnishings for our new home in West Hartford, as Allan found a job there. He passed the New York Bar exam and the Connecticut Bar, so he could practice law in either state. He promised to look for a job in New York City, but I believe he spent most summer afternoons in movie theaters. He was tired of being in the city, and he wanted to live where there was green grass, a quick and easy work commute, and many connections. His parents lived in West Hartford. Allan's dad was a physician, and he and Allan's mother knew many professional people in the Hartford area. In just one afternoon of looking for a job in Connecticut, he landed a position as a subrogation lawyer for Aetna Insurance Company.

I was apprehensive and couldn't fathom moving away from New York, especially from my family, but since Allan's folks lived in Connecticut, he'd be able to tap into that social network for business if we relocated. I liked his parents and the idea of living in a small town grew on me. I hoped we would move back to New York in a few years.

Time went by fast. My mom convinced me to take an elective course in typing during my last year of high school. I was glad I did. I found an office job working at the drama school where I studied, which allowed me to take acting courses without paying tuition. What a bonus!

Mom and I developed a congenial and close relationship in the year before my marriage. I knew Mom didn't want me to move to another state, but it tapped into her daring spirit. She was supportive. My dad complained about our leaving New York from the day he learned about Allan's job at Aetna, until the day I left my parents' home to drive the two-and-a-half hours to West Hartford.

I left my job several weeks before my wedding. We planned to honeymoon in Canada, and I needed some time to pack and say a proper goodbye to family and friends. Though I was hesitant about moving, I was also excited about the prospect of having a great life with a man who would do everything to make things as pleasant as possible for me. He appreciated my willingness to move to Connecticut. He knew how much I loved the city, and recognized all the pressure my dad was putting on me. My father was unyielding about our living in New York. He made it clear that the "right" apartment was available in our building.

Moving day arrived, and my parents walked us to the car to say farewell. I assured them that we were moving just a few hours away. We would visit every other weekend. They also had the option of taking the train to see us. Our new apartment had an extra bedroom to accommodate out-of-town guests, which I reminded my folks.

My stomach was in knots; I had trouble eating during the previous few weeks. I lost ten pounds. I was sure I forgot something important. It was late fall, my favorite time of year. We could see the park from the front of our building where we were standing. The trees were ablaze in my preferred colors: burgundy, gold, and bright orange. It was early in the morning, and New York looked more magnificent than ever. No traffic. Few people. I didn't want to leave the excitement of this ideal place, nor did I want to leave my family. Mom and Dad always made me feel that life revolved around my being near them.

We hugged my folks and said we'd phone when we got settled in our new flat. As I was getting into the car, my dad tapped me on my shoulder. He couldn't speak. Tears welled up in his eyes. You would've thought I was moving to Europe. He said, "I don't know how I will manage without you." It was the first time I ever saw my dad cry. My mother gave Dad a look and walked away. I knew how she felt by her quick pace and straight back. I saw the anger in her stiff shoulders. Dad made me feel bad on a day she wanted me to have peace. Mom was reassuring about my leaving the city to be with the man I loved. I knew she was sad, but she had her life and wouldn't intrude on mine. I was speechless. I couldn't move. I looked at my dad, dapper as ever in his three-piece suit, and I finally said, "You and Mom will be fine."

I got into the car and Allan reached over and kissed me. "I am sorry that you have to go through such anguish leaving New York to move to our new home." I started to sob and didn't stop until we reached New Haven.

8

Comrades and Companions

"Everyone is doing the best they can at any given moment, and when they can do differently, they will." Virginia Satir never said this to me directly, but she told me, and several hundred other people at an American Association of Marriage and Family Therapy conference, this simple phrase, which made so much sense to me when I heard it after becoming a psychologist. I wish the wisdom in this saying was clearer to me when I married Allan on October 21, 1956. I was 18, and he was 26.

We had a mutual physical attraction, and we had a friendship. We enjoyed doing many of the same things. It might have been a walk on the beach, old movies, musicals, Chinese food, or spending time with our families. We realized later in our marriage that happily married couples aren't psychologically more perceptive than others. They are not more affluent or more attractive. What makes a marriage compelling is amazingly basic, not at all a mystery. They are partners and they are independent at the same time. Along with enjoying each other's company, couples learn to keep their negative feelings from overpowering their positive ones. That's the key issue and can take many years to learn.

I gave the appearance of being sophisticated and mature, but I was uninformed and naïve.

I wanted to marry Allan, and I was eager to leave my home, specifically my life with my parents.

Moving to Connecticut, away from my family, friends, and the pulse of the city that I knew and loved so dearly, gave me the most profound feeling of isolation. Allan's father thought I was too young to be married and didn't approve. He thought that I was a clever child. In many ways, I was. Allan's mother loved me from the start and was happy that we lived near her in West Hartford. She and I became close and spoke by telephone every day. However, this still didn't change things for me. I felt like an alien. I didn't belong. I was a trespasser in some foreign city, only two hours away.

What kind of work could I do? I had a background in theater. I took a college preparatory course in high school. Once again, the typing course I was convinced to take in high school came in handy. I found a job as a secretary for the president of a real estate company. What nerve I had! My training to be an actress at The American Academy of Dramatic Arts during high school is what landed me the job. I truly bluffed my way into the position, but I worked hard and stayed for two years.

It was a large firm, and I enjoyed the people. I left when my daughter Janet was born.

I missed the theater. There were some live performances in downtown Hartford at the Bushnell Theater, but I was a New York City theater snob and looked upon these shows as amateurish. I knew I had to find a drama coach and return to what I enjoyed most in life (other than my family). I started studying with a wonderful teacher who owned a studio in West Hartford, and she became my director and my friend. She was honest, nurturing, and supportive. I was fortunate to have her in my life when my mother died very suddenly at 57 from a coronary thrombosis. Janet was a year and a half. I was crushed and went into a deep depression. It wasn't fair; my mother and I just started to get along. We spoke by telephone daily and no longer argued. I became phobic; my hands would shake. There were many days when I called Allan to come home from his office. Shortly after my mother passed away, I had another daughter, Rachel. My depression became even worse. I just couldn't cope.

Allan was panicked. He never showed his fear openly, but I felt it. It was tough for him to interrupt his life during the day, and come home to a depressed wife. Allan didn't want to be a caretaker like his mother was to his father. He needed to count on me. He wanted a companion and a partner. I knew he loved me; he wanted me to be more independent and less depressed. I didn't know if I could accomplish what seemed like an overwhelming task.

My despair didn't go away. For a while, I performed at

home the way I acted on stage. I did household chores; I took care of my family. We were social; we entertained, we went out with friends and had Sunday dinner with Allan's family. I presented a visual fairytale to the outside world, truly fiction. I hired a babysitter. When I was alone, I was in bed and in tears. I slept whenever free time permitted, and my dreams, my fantasies, and my expectations were all negative.

Allan's dad was manic-depressive and was constantly in and out of hospitals. Allan's mom, a wealthy woman, travelled with her husband, hoping he'd get better. It didn't work, and Allan's dad couldn't work. He wouldn't leave his bed for days and stopped practicing medicine. He would enter a hospital and his stay would last a few weeks. He underwent shock treatments; medication for mental illness was almost non-existent in the early 1960s. During that extended bout battling mental illness, Allan's dad worked in a factory until he was well enough to go back to his medical practice. Watching this brilliant doctor, reduced in status to counting screws in a machine shop because of mental illness, took its toll on the family.

A psychiatrist told the family to leave his dad, or he would never improve. A separation seemed to be the only solution, followed by a divorce, when Allan was 13. The family moved to New York City with his mother and two siblings. Allan's folks remarried when Allan was 21. To be divorced during the 1940s was difficult for his brave and caring mother, for any woman during that era no matter what the reason. Eventually, Allan's father was well enough to return to practicing medicine.

Allan indeed had many connections in our small Connecticut town; he established a busy law practice. He left the insurance company, and eventually left law to go into real estate. My brother Yale's elevator business flourished in New York and he wanted to invest his profits in a new venture. Allan found the perfect building in Hartford and convinced my brother to invest his money. Allan ultimately became a partner and developed a talent for restoring and reconstructing old established buildings.

My depression wouldn't go away. I couldn't share feelings with Allan or anyone. Minor issues seemed like major crises. If dinner didn't turn out well, I became upset. If our daughter was cranky, it was my fault. If the house didn't look the way I thought it should, it was my failure and my mistake.

I didn't have an easy time being a parent. I wanted to be more loving and caring than my mother, who was critical and hard to please. I loved my two beautiful, sweet girls, but I felt a great deal of pressure. As a family, we drove to New York City at least once a month to see plays and visit with my parents and friends. Allan also rushed home at least twice a week to make dinner for the children so I could attend my drama classes. That ended very soon, as my beloved drama coach was diagnosed with lung cancer and didn't have long to live. My coach's death added to my sadness and depression. I was anorexic, barely ate, didn't see friends, wouldn't return phone calls, and cried myself to sleep.

I was worried about my marriage. I didn't grasp the significance of why Allan distanced himself from me. He thought I might be like his father. I was desperate. I knew I needed help and didn't know where to turn. I went to a family physician to ask for the name of a psychiatrist. As the physician took my blood pressure, he put my hand on his erect penis. I started to cry, and he didn't know what to do. He apologized profusely, gave me the name of a psychiatrist, and rushed me out of his office. The psychiatrist was as unethical as the physician. He said that I probably flirted with my family physician. He was a 60-year-old doctor and I was 24. Flirting? I was so depressed I couldn't even flirt with my husband. I went to both "professionals" only once.

I eventually found an analyst. This profound man convinced me to get involved in local theater, and ultimately, take some college courses. I joined a new theater company, "Theatre off the Green," and played the character roles that hadn't been available to me very often in the past. I was the prostitute in "J.B." (*The Book of Job*) that summer and earned rave reviews. The local theater gave me the opportunity to choose character parts as well as the usual ingénue parts. I played my typical role in *Dear Charles*, a fun comedy. I changed my mindset about summer stock and community theater. I liked the people. Most of the folks in these plays were down-to-earth and hard workers. They held different occupations during the day and would come to rehearsals in the evenings. Some of the actors were stay-at-home parents, as I was, and this theater group was their relaxation and diversion. I appreciated my time with my new friends, and the following fall I got involved with two other theater groups, one in Windsor, Connecticut, and one in Springfield, Massachusetts. I never studied set design and costumes extensively in drama school, but I became involved in these areas at both theaters. I travelled to professional costume houses in New York. I learned how to build sets from written plans. I became friendly with three of the directors, and they taught me all they could about directing. When I learned that the person who directed plays at the local community college was ill, I applied for the position and got it. I directed three plays for the school, and I felt a deep humility and appreciation for those around me. I strengthened myself and my relationships. My family benefited. My children thrived, and my husband seemed happy.

My mother-in-law died of a heart attack during this time. Allan's father became very ill again. Being a physician, he felt guilty that he hadn't recognized his wife's symptoms. I became close to him over the years, and we invited him to live with us. We decided to add another room and bath to our home. We hired the contractors Allan was using to renovate his buildings to do the work. Within six weeks of his wife's death, my father-in-law had a stroke and died. We decided to continue with our plan to enlarge our house, and I got the idea to make a theater in our basement and start a drama school. Allan was as enthusiastic as I was, and within three months we had a full basement theater with a proscenium arch, a backstage dressing room, and great lighting. It was a first-rate theater that would seat 200 people. To have a drama school in my home, where I could teach and be near my children, was appealing and challenging.

In retrospect, the pearl of wisdom in Virginia Satir's insightful spoken words started to make sense to me, although I wasn't aware of this brilliant therapist/educator at that period in my life. I'd been doing the best I could until I might do differently. Up until that juncture, my childhood injuries interfered with my mental health and hindered my marriage. A good relationship and positive parenting weren't instinctive to me. I didn't have the expertise to make matrimonial harmony. Most people acquire marriage skills from watching parents and friends interact. My folks were not people to imitate. They were not a team, and they did not communicate. I tried doing everything the opposite of what they'd done, and in the process became overwhelmed and depressed.

My analyst helped me realize that making mistakes was part of the learning process. If my life was going to change, I needed to shed my perfectionist tendencies in everything I did. I also needed to communicate what I wanted to Allan and persuade him to feel secure enough to share what he needed from me. There were no magical answers, no immediate improvements. Eventually, I became a happier person and more independent, and these changes finally transformed the complexities of our family.

9

Passion in the Basement

My drama school opened and had a promising start. I had a cool, calm spirit, with tightly crossed fingers. I scheduled five weekly classes, and they were full. There was interest and not much competition. The Hartford Conservatory had a few classes mixed with music, but my school was unique to the area since it focused on improvisation and scene study. Viola Spolin's improvisational theater book was my companion.

I volunteered as a drama coach in the north end of Hartford six months before opening my facility. Schools in Hartford had meager resources. I wanted some of the kids in my classes. The thought of having all suburban youngsters and adults in my basement was as unpleasant to me as moving to Connecticut when I first married Allan. I knew many young people from Hartford couldn't afford the tuition the suburbanites paid, but I thought paying something was important. I remembered the early '50s, when Maria Ley-Piscator, my first drama coach, charged a dollar a week. I did the same for city kids.

We had a capable, diversified group of people at my house every week. I planned the classes in advance but never looked at the plan. I was as improvisational as my guru, Viola Spolin. Two groups of 10 to 12-year-olds met once a week after school. They were excited about acting, the connections with their old friends, and the new young people they met. Their chatter filled my house from the moment I opened the door until well after the class was over and I needed to politely tell them to go home. There were two classes for 13 to 17-year-olds; one group met in the afternoon, but many of the girls worked after school and still wanted to be involved. Several of the girls chided me into starting an evening class for teenagers. Adult men and women also gathered one night a week. They had no desire to memorize lines but liked reading scenes from plays aloud. Several romances blossomed from those weekly readings. A divorced man and newly separated mother of three started dating at the end of our first session together. They ultimately married.

My classes were all wait-listed.

The summer before opening my school, I acted in different theater groups. I played a wide range of roles in *Look Homeward Angel, A Thurber's Carnival, Solid Gold Cadillac, Cat on a Hot Tin Roof*, and my most favorite, *Laura*. The theater editor of one of the local newspapers became my leading supporter. Leo Smith loved all types of theater and the arts and reviewed every play. He was exuberant about promoting goodwill in the theater world and wrote high-quality reviews. Leo was excited about any new "happening" in the Greater Hartford area. He was a treasure to the three directors, who started "Theater off the Green," which was also my first involvement in community theater. Leo came to the premiere performance of *The Seven Year Itch*, where I played one of the protagonist's fantasy girls, Miss Morris. He gave the play a rave review. Leo occupied the same seat in the second row at every opening of every play that summer.

I was a "groupie" once again. I participated in most aspects of community theater. I was in all the plays, but if the role wasn't demanding, I also handled public relations. I created the costumes for *A Thurber's Carnival*. I painted scenery. I was around most of my free time. I learned some valuable skills that would help me with my new endeavor.

Leo visited during the day to watch the stagehands build the sets, and meet and talk to the actors and directors. Leo and I became fast friends. I called him when my basement theater was ready for classes, and he came out with a photographer who took pictures. My new theater was exceptional, and could also have become an apartment, if necessary. The backstage dressing room was a hub. The students congregated there as soon as they arrived to apply makeup and try on my vintage shop costumes. This room had four walls and a door. Another similar space had a significant storage area for props, costumes, and small pieces of furniture. There was a full bath for the students and guests. The lighting board was substantial. The raised platform stage with its wood floor and automatic curtain could have evolved into a living room. We carpeted the space, other than the stage, in red, to coordinate with the red curtain. The walls were light oak paneling. My home theater was striking, and I had gratuitous publicity. Leo was a city guy and liked the concept of my school.

At the end of the first year, we put on a production for 200 guests. The students all performed. We chose *A Final Dress Rehearsal*, which was a play within a play, for the younger group. This group of all girls tried to put on *Cinderella*. They made mistakes, as the play was about putting on a play, and the errors were part of the presentation. Missing a line or two, or even a short scene, made the girls laugh. The audience had as much fun as they did.

The older girls were dedicated, doing scenes from Tennessee Williams, Thomas Wolfe, Arthur Miller, and William Shakespeare. It was a superb evening. I received encouragement from the community and continued with my classes for the next three years. I was proud of what we were accomplishing.

Drama classes met after school and in the evenings. My children were in school all day, and I had ample free time. Planning for my classes took a few hours. I could no longer be in a production since most rehearsals were after work and would interfere with my teaching. This junction was perfect for starting college. I registered for two courses at the University of Harford. We hired Tessa, a lovely young woman from San Salvador, to help with the laundry, grocery shopping, and cleaning. I couldn't comfortably juggle college courses, teaching, and family responsibilities.

I wanted more time with my girls and my husband, so I gave up most of my drama classes to begin a new passion, college. I always wanted more education, and this was the right time. I became enthusiastic about each course. The professors became my directors and my classmates my co-actors. I stopped teaching drama, but I knew that I would eventually go back to it in some form.

10

Among Other Things

Everything Allan did influenced me, and similarly, my behavior affected him and our relationship. I was home-based and more available now. He was satisfied with our current arrangement. It was a good time for us and our marriage. Teaching drama kept me home, but I was habitually occupied.

I now did things with my daughters that I didn't for the last few years. I drove carpools, I became a "brownie leader," a room mother, and an ice skater. I started cooking and followed recipes. Teaching drama often conflicted with our dinner hour. Meals became as improvisational as drama classes. Dinner was frequently boxed or take-out food from local restaurants. I surprised my family with some of my creations. Hamburger Helper was no longer from a box. Coq au vin was called Mom's chicken and took me hours to prepare.

I became a devoted college student at the University of Hartford. I registered for two courses for my first semester. I took an English Literature course during the day with Scott Brown, an articulate professor, who inspired my interest in John Keats. He read poetry the way John Gielgud recited Hamlet's soliloquy. My first college paper was "Ode on a Grecian Urn." It was memorable to me because I got an A+. It was a good start for my initial college course. I am still friendly with Scott and his partner, Jon. We have the same taste in restaurants and movies and run into each other probably five times a year.

The other course was in the evening, Western Civilization with Gabe Jones. Gabe was the first African-American history teacher in West Hartford. He taught at Conard High School during the day and was an adjunct professor at night. His history course was the story of humanity and human affairs. He wasn't concerned about dates. He inspired the dullest imagination. He became one of my closest friends and the most ardent advocate of my drama school. His daughter was one of my drama students.

After the first semester, I registered for four courses and continued full-time until I earned a degree in communications and drama. I studied every psychology course that was available and thought I might eventually bring the study of dramatic arts to a different setting, perhaps a high school. I took some method courses so I could teach if I decided to go that route.

Allan became captivated with skiing and thought this was a good time to buy a house in Vermont. Janet and Rachel were tweens and equally charmed by the sport. We bought a house in Stratton with my brother Yale and his family. I wasn't happy sharing a house with another family, even my brother's. There wasn't a comfortable situation for all of us to stay together at one time, and I was afraid that we'd run into conflicts. We bought it, nevertheless. Grateful for all the reinforcement I was getting in all areas of my life, I decided to let the two men work out the details. Stratton was a nice place to spend weekends doing school work and learning to ski. We loved the house, and five years later bought my brother's share. Some problems arose, since Allan let many of our friends and business acquaintances use the house when we weren't there. I never knew what surprises we would find when we arrived, including people who thought they could extend their stay without letting us know.

Until this time in my life, I never enjoyed flying. I loved to travel but flew reluctantly. Getting on a plane was never an easy task for me. It didn't stop me from going places, and with a glass of wine for courage, I could fly anywhere. Flying was exciting for Allan, and he decided to take lessons and buy a plane with our friend. He convinced me to take lessons. I got as far as finishing ground school when he crashed a new plane. The motor conked out; the plane turned over. He was lucky to be alive. I quit. I started taking golf lessons during the summer in Vermont, thinking I could interest Allan in this dull sport, and perhaps he would give up flying. I did have some fun, but it wasn't fast enough for me. I took tennis lessons before learning golf, and immediately valued that sport. It was a fast way to get a good workout. In an hour, I got more exercise playing tennis than four hours on a golf course. I wasn't good at golf, either. Allan was a natural athlete and became an accomplished golfer. We would occasionally play together, but he started playing with the guys. It got me off the hook. I had a year left in college before I graduated and was thinking about graduate schools.

My dad, who was a constant guest, came up for a week during the spring of 1973. He visited me at least once a month. We always got along. I started to notice how he became critical of me on the day he was going home. He complained about my enrollment in school. "Why would you do anything difficult when Allan is so successful? You should be home with your children." After a while, I figured it out. He loved my family and his time with us, so he had a hard time saying goodbye. I told him that he could leave whenever he wanted, and we wouldn't argue any longer on his last day visiting. He didn't understand what he was doing. It took me a while. He just turned 75, and my brothers and I threw a party for him at the Plaza Hotel in New York, close to where he lived. We invited his relatives. It was a large clan, and they all came. I never saw my dad this surprised and happy.

Shortly after his birthday, Dad's visit was different. When he was ready to leave, he was amicable. I think he was anxious to go home and see his doctor. He showed me his ankle, which was twice the size of the other. He said he wasn't feeling well. I didn't want him to go home alone without being checked out by my doctor first. We went to the emergency room, met my physician, and the doctor admitted my dad. The staff told him that he had a gall bladder problem and he needed surgery.

It was pancreatic cancer. He never left the hospital. I spent two months at his side doing school work and feeling helpless.

Two weeks after my dad was diagnosed with cancer, Allan had a massive coronary. It was the eve of his 42nd birthday. Both men were in the same hospital at the same time. My children were thirteen and ten. Allan lost 40 percent of his heart. I was devastated. So were the girls. A week after Allan's heart attack, my brother, Don, was told he had an aortic valve problem and would require open heart surgery. He had just married Bessie, a woman he met in California. Even though I was more grounded than when my mother died, I never felt so alone. My other brother, Yale, had a complicated life at that time and wasn't available to me. My closest friend in Hartford, Enid, was my support system and listened to my fears and helped me as much as she could. She had three children and had a husband with a heart problem. We met when Enid moved to Connecticut from Chicago. My daughter, Janet, and Enid's youngest daughter, Holly, went to nursery school together. She is my closest friend to this day. The other person who listened with incredible patience was Gabe Jones, my good friend, and history teacher.

One of the saddest days of my life was witnessing Allan get out of a wheelchair near my dad's room on the day Allan was leaving the hospital. He went to say good-bye to my dad. We never told Dad his diagnoses, and never told Dad about Allan's heart attack. They kept things from patients in the '70s. Dad died the next day. Allan couldn't attend his funeral. My father became the dad that Allan never had. They bonded over real estate and Allan's work. They stayed up talking for hours while the rest of us slept.

I graduated college that year, and other than the birth of my children, that was the happiest day of my life. I had more fear walking across that stage to receive my degree (Summa Cum Laude, I might boastfully add) than I had ever experienced in any of the roles I'd played. I always had butterflies before going on stage, but never to this extent. My family and friends were all at my graduation, and Allan had a party for me in celebration. School was a satisfying part of my life and I was going to continue my education.

Allan was stoic. He was young to have had a serious heart attack, and he never complained. He refused to let any physical ailment stop him from doing the things he wanted to do. He was no longer permitted to fly a plane, but he played golf and started collecting coins (which took him all over the country), skied all winter in Vermont and out West, and said it was time to buy another house with a pool. He wanted to swim every day to stay strong. He found a beautiful home while the girls and I were in Florida, and with our permission (he was persuasive) bought the house. I wasn't pleased. Our lifestyle changed. The girls went to a fine public school in West Hartford, and with the move, that would end. We moved to Bloomfield in the middle of the school year and decided to put them in private school. I was never a private school enthusiast, but we didn't want to compromise our children's education. We needed live-in help, as the house was too large for me to manage and was a full-time job. Being in real estate, Allan knew a good buy when he saw one. He had to have this house and used the pool and health as his rationale. How could I say no?

We struggled to keep our lives from changing, but there is no way to arrest the course of change. It's not a matter of whether you choose to change, but how you do it. Our lives changed drastically, and I cannot say for the better.

11

Personal Expectations

We grow up with a list of beliefs that shape our lives. To a large extent, our careers, relationships, hopes, and dreams, are based on what occurred during our childhood. Our parents' behavior clearly sharpened our inclinations, our standards, and our personal expectations. What we witnessed in the homes of our peers, what we read in books, viewed in plays, movies, and on television, supplemented our perceptions of ourselves and eventually our marital relationships.

I had a problematic childhood with parents who didn't communicate. I saw myself as a fortunate adult married to a remarkable man. Allan was an involved and supportive parent, a great provider, and a caring and loving husband. He had a fun side that was therapeutic to all of us as our daughters were growing up. When he had his first heart attack, Janet and Rachel bought Allan "Henry." This adorable, fuzzy stuffed animal looked like a yellow "Snoopy." It came in all sizes and was the "Dear

Abby" of our household. Allan collected these little animals. They had different and distinctive vocal sounds. The girls told Henry their problems, Henry answered in one of Allan's remarkable voices. I think our daughters even made up situations to laugh at themselves. Al Gore stayed at our house during a fundraiser and saw the Henry collection. Gore sent Allan a "Tennessee-Henry," guitar and all. Allan's Southern Henry voice was hilarious. He had a terrible accent.

I believe Allan was convinced, regarding mental health, that he married a woman like his father, who was anything but mentally healthy. I was loved, but treated like a fragile doll, maybe not a stuffed doll, but one who needed to be held up and pampered. I asked Allan, numerous times, to go to counseling with me because we saw the world so differently. Our values were similar, but I looked deeply into all issues, and he stayed on the surface. After much cajoling, he went once. He said to the psychologist/marriage counselor, "I am fine, our marriage is great. My wife suggests that I had a difficult childhood, like hers. I had a wonderful childhood." Allan's dad was in and out of mental hospitals for most of his growing-up years.

I was an excitable, hot-blooded woman in every area of my life. I was far from the calm, low-keyed exterior that would have described Allan. I got emotional, cried in the movies, became hysterical whenever Allan had a heart problem, and was frightened at the thought of losing him, either by death or to another woman. At one stage of our lives, I asked him if he wanted a divorce. He looked at me as if I were crazy and said, "Why, aren't you happy?"

Over the years, I believe I did a good deal of growing and changing. I'm not sure he noticed. We seldom argued, and we did many things together, particularly as a family. We also did many things separately. We traveled during school vacations with Janet and Rachel. We went to Europe, to golf resorts and spas. Allan became an avid golfer, and we joined a country club. He would often have dinner at this club and use the restaurant and golf course to entertain guests and business associates. Allan became involved in politics. He called himself a Republican, but Libertarian would better characterize his views if he were living today. He ultimately got involved with the Democratic Party and became an Ambassador to the Gilbert Islands. We did a good deal of traveling with the Democratic Party folks, and the people were fun, from all walks of life.

Allan never complained about having anything physically wrong with him, and he looked like the poster person for fitness and health. He was handsome and he aged well. He never lost his hair, and it was as blonde as the day I met him. He was grateful to be alive after several bouts with death. He was compelled to share his success with those in need, both men and women. The men never gave me a problem, but the women were a bone of contention. When his secretary wanted to open a restaurant but didn't have the finances, Allan became her benefactor. When a waitress at the country club wanted to go to nursing school but couldn't afford the tuition,

Allan was the fairy godparent who gave her money. The hostess at a favorite restaurant lived in a marginal section of town; Guess who helped her find a new place? Allan was a guardian angel to many people, and I was proud of him. But the women did give me a dilemma.

My goal was to be as supportive a wife as possible and to communicate. It was equally important for me to work toward a rewarding career, one that would take me into my senior years and maintain my interest. I received my Master's in Counseling from the University of Hartford the same year Janet entered Loomis Chaffee School in Windsor. Rachel was an eighth grader at Kingswood-Oxford Middle School. We often did our homework together and talked about how lucky we were that Allan had three years of uninterrupted good health.

When I was completing my second Master's in Family Therapy at Saint Joseph's College, Allan had bypass surgery and came through it well, but lost more of his heart function. The doctors felt that he had a silent heart attack sometime prior to surgery. Janet entered her second year at The College of the Holy Cross in Worcester, Massachusetts. Rachel was now at Loomis Chaffee School and living at home. The girls could have attended school anywhere, but they liked being nearby. Allan's heart issue gave me and the girls anxiety. He existed as if he was in perfect health, and never slowed down for a moment. We hired Adele as a housekeeper. She lived and worked for us while attending school part-time to study art. A helpful presence in our home, she became an important part of our family.

I took a Psychotherapy course at the University of Hartford and learned about Psychodrama. By the time I finished my degree at Saint Joseph's College, I received my Psychodrama certification. What a wonderful career change for me. I used my dramatic background and my newly acquired curiosity in an incredible field of psychology. Psychodrama is a form of therapy that saves hours of therapeutic time for the patient, called the protagonist. I spent many days in Beacon, New York, and some week nights in New Haven, studying this fascinating discipline.

I tried to coax Allan to join me in Beacon at an open Psychodrama evening. I explained that Psychodrama was acting. We would closely reestablish life situations and act them out in the present. He could be part of the audience. He didn't have to participate. Clients have the freedom to figure out their behavior and more deeply understand a situation in their lives. "We could use this method to gain an awareness of our marriage," I said. I was foolish to mention anything to do with our lives. Allan was a very private person and I imagine this idea scared him. He had no desire to join me at that time, or ever.

For me, understanding a condition in real time, and eventually using this method in a variety of clinical and community-based settings, was mind boggling. We perform this type of therapy in a group setting, but it is not group therapy; it's an individual psychotherapy that people perform within a group. The idea is like the memoir concept of "show me, don't tell me." There is an audience, and the people in the audience volunteer to become therapeutic representatives for one another's scenes. The protagonist focuses on a situation which is enacted on stage. It could be a memory, a dream, or fantasy. It might be preparation for a future circumstance, or some unfinished business. Members of the group or audience become the auxiliaries and reinforce the protagonist by playing significant roles in the scene: an alter-ego, a parent, a child, a boss. A psychodrama is guided by the director, a person trained in the technique. We condense therapy that would take weeks into an hour-and-a-half session. The protagonist is encouraged to be spontaneous and creative and can use any prop or costume that would help the client/ protagonist with restorative healing.

Many of the people on this stage, who bore their souls to a group of strangers, had as much to say as Arthur Miller or John Steinbeck. I became certified and found a part-time job in an inner-city school in Hartford. I worked with a group of young men who were just released from a juvenile correctional institute. One young man took out a handgun as his prop. Allan convinced me to leave that job.

After I completed my Master's in Family Therapy at Saint Joseph's College and found an internship working with alcoholic and drug rehabilitation at the UConn Health Center, I realized how little I knew about addiction. I wanted to take one more course in "Altered States of Consciousness." This undergraduate course was through Central Connecticut State College and ran for two weeks during the summer for three hours each day. I met a man in that class who was starting college. We were the only two adults in the class, and this was his first course. He was a musician, a drummer, having just returned from New Orleans to his mother's home in New Britain. I must have put out a sign or signal that stated: "Let me take care of you." We had lunch together and I became his "therapist" as well as his friend. Most of his buddies were musicians and had moved to other areas. He was lonely. I was fascinated with this man. He was a hairdresser and a drummer and couldn't find a place for himself in either sphere. I invited him to our home for dinner and thought it would be good for him to meet my family. It was summertime, the girls were home, and Fred told them tales about his life in New Orleans. He lived in a house that was run by a Madam. He was her maintenance man, and he didn't hesitate to describe his wide-ranging responsibilities. Allan was bewildered by my friendship with Fred. We were so different. He was outspoken about his views on legalizing drugs, politics, and his religion. He had many problems, and I convinced him to come with me to The Moreno (Psychodrama) Institute in Beacon.

Fred was the first person I directed that I knew before entering the psychodrama theater. Before Fred, the protagonists with whom I worked were strangers. With my direction and assistance from people in the audience, Fred viewed his life clearly. His father left the family when Fred was a boy, and the church replaced his father. He felt guilty about joining the Navy, becoming a musician, and leaving his mother. He realized why he decided to travel to Connecticut and enroll in college. He wanted to care for his mom. She was getting older. The nearby university was his justification to live with her.

Even though we had little in common, we became friends. He spent some evenings at our house, and my family made him comfortable, but he made them uncomfortable. He was opinionated and verbal and talked about issues that didn't interest my family, usually people. I realized time with Fred should happen in other venues such as school or at lunch. No more home visits.

It was soon after his evening at the Moreno Institute that I realized I wanted something different, another form of drama. I decided to pursue a Ph.D. in Clinical Psychology. I started the next year after I finished my internship at the UConn Health Center. Allan and the girls were pleased to see me back at school and close to home. For a few years, I stayed out of other people's lives, I no longer directed nor counseled.

12

In the Beginning

It was June 1980, and I just received my Doctorate in Counseling Psychology. I was eager to hang out my shingle and open my office. I found a perfect place. It had two large rooms in a small building in the center of Bloomfield, a medium-sized town close to downtown Hartford, five minutes from home. Allan said, "It is not what you have that counts, but what people think you have that counts." He suggested that I buy impressive furnishings and have a private waiting room with two doors, one door leading into the office and another door out of my office, into the hallway. He thought it might be a good idea for people to avoid one another in the waiting room. If Allan's contractor was able to do the work, the owner of the building was on board.

Decorating was fun and inspiring.

I took more time selecting wall décor than choosing furniture. I believe that people can be fascinated by provocative art and that certain items can serve as conversation starters for reticent patients. Hundreds of years ago, when many people couldn't read, paintings were sometimes designed to draw out the life stories of observers. I found some colorful and interesting lithographs. People have always debated about art – how to make it, what it signifies. Some think paintings should be representational, but many artists generate more innovative works, especially since we have great technology to record exactly how things look. People can more easily discuss Georgia O'Keeffe's "Black Iris" than the troubles in their marriage. I chose several of O'Keeffe's flower paintings – roses, lilies, and weeds. The flowers were so large, some 15 times life size, that not everyone could distinguish them. The idea that O'Keeffe's work was innately feminine only came up with some folks, but most talked about the shape, the dark colors, and the gloomy characteristics.

I went to my office the first Saturday after opening to hang some pictures. I put a few nails in the wall to hang my degrees and certificates. I tried to hook up an interesting painting of "Masks" – by an unknown artist that I picked up in a New York shop – in the waiting room. This painting eventually had people of all ages curious. Most people tried to figure out the difference between sadness and depression, which is what the masks represented most.

The psychological aspects of the artwork and the artist became a fundamental topic for many, but more people debated the distinguishing characteristics of sadness and depression. The consensus seemed to be that depression is an emotional state of despair, a mental illness with many symptoms, while sadness is not. When we feel depressed, we feel unmotivated. We are unable to concentrate, and cannot complete basic tasks. We feel hopeless. It is a disheartened feeling that includes pain. By comparison, sadness is a human condition, a natural reaction to painful situations, which is not as debilitating as depression.

When I went to hang the artwork, I couldn't get the nail on the wall. I was not very handy. I thought I was having a problem with my hammer. I knocked on my neighbor's door and asked him if he had a hammer I could borrow since mine wasn't working. George laughed, brought his hammer to my office and carefully hung the painting for me.

"You were hitting a beam," he said. "Nothing wrong with your tool, but I am happy to help, and love the painting." He had some time and offered to hang the rest of my artwork.

I was enthusiastic about a large subway poster that I found myself staring at for long periods of time, always seeing something I hadn't seen before. I hoped that the poster would offer a similar type of stimulation to my patients. In the picture, people were going about their lives, on the way to someplace, creating personal space for themselves in a crowded subway. Folks were dressed formally, or casually, holding unusual objects. It was interesting to examine the observers' reactions to the activities within the artwork. Many patients weren't aware that they'd be providing me with insight into their beliefs and thought processes, and I would often start a session with their perceptions.

George and I found the right spot for it, above the coffee table in front of the large couch, also in the waiting room. He enjoyed gazing at it as much as I did.

Jackson Pollock's drip painting elicited talk of color, texture, and his wild dynamic energy. George and I spent half of an hour trying to figure out the inner workings of his mind. Why did Pollock start painting enormous abstract pictures by dripping and splashing paint? It was a far-fetched change from portraying recognizable objects to a completely different style. Pollock perforated paint cans and swayed them over his canvas. Sometimes he added sand and glass for texture. He believed art should be a way of communicating emotional states. George and I enjoyed chatting about this painting, and patients often wanted to talk about what they viewed; their observations often broke the ice.

The blue, rust, and white color-coordinated furniture in the waiting room was comfortable. I often had to explain to patients that I wouldn't mind having them unwind in my office for a few hours before their session, but pointed out that they might bump into a co-worker or a neighbor, someone who might value privacy. People enjoyed being there. The room easily accommodated a family of eight or a group of business executives.

Patients and other tenants in the building used a bathroom that was outside my office. My lavatory had a hotplate, a refrigerator, and a sink, but I decided not to share it. When I first opened my office, I allowed a man to use the lavatory, and I believe he fell asleep. I was going to be late for my next client, so I knocked on the door, and the man said, "I'll be out in a minute." Ten minutes later he left the bathroom and entered my office, 15 minutes into the next session where another client was in tears. How would it have been for these two people if they had known each other? It was an invasion of their privacy. That proved the end of sharing my bathroom with anyone.

I chose the same color scheme for the waiting room and my office. If the gathering was larger than usual, I moved chairs back and forth, and everything seemed to belong. I covered the walls to my office with a wide range of fine art, drawings, paintings, and sculpture behind glass. People favored "Modern Life" by Andrew Wyeth and Grant Wood's "American Gothic." Diplomas and my clinical membership to different organizations were behind my desk. I wanted to enjoy spending seven or eight hours a day in this workplace. I often fantasized that I could spend a week crashing there during a snowstorm and be quite content. People came to my office and felt comfortable.

While George was hanging my paintings, we talked about theater and the arts in general. He told me that he had just started a computer business with several partners, and he said, "I am going through a horrible divorce which should be final any day." He invited me to lunch, and I learned that he was a professional cellist, as well as a computer programmer.

George was a workaholic. I believe it was his way of

covering up the pain he was feeling about his divorce. Whenever George had a free moment and I was not seeing a patient, he visited and spent time looking at the paintings and admiring my office. It was a tranquil space. I spent 35 remarkable years there.

13

Therapist, Heal Thyself

I decided to introduce myself to the community. I gave a free workshop on parenting skills at a local junior high school. Who wouldn't be interested in becoming a better parent? I met a broad spectrum of people in the area, and many had problems that went beyond parenting. I saw at least one-third of this group as patients.

I was also fortunate to have many physicians as friends, and they were generous with referrals. There was a new restaurant about two minutes from my office, and one of the owners also ran the human resource department at Cigna Insurance Company. I ate lunch there almost every day. He introduced himself to me and was an incredible help in sending clients. Within three months of opening my office, I had 30 patients. I was in the process of becoming licensed and worked with Alfred Levy, a psychiatrist in New Haven, to complete my intern hours. I met Alfred at an open psychodrama evening and he asked me to come work for him. It was an hour drive, and too far. I wanted an office a few minutes from home and a solo practice. He offered to consult with me about my patients and sign their insurance forms until I received my license. People wanted reimbursement.

Two patients with whom I began to work on a weekly basis started therapy the Monday after my opening. I wondered, *who are these people and how do they think? How will I be able to motivate them to best resolve their problems? Can I be the agent to assist people to make the changes that they need to make them successful and happy?* These are several of the questions that I considered, and still do.

Being a mentor, I believe it is vital to put the onus on what people want and to help them support themselves. During my training and my internship, I became familiar with many ideas and methods of formidable thinkers in psychology to try and figure out the mystery of human thought, emotion, and behavior. It was Carl Rogers, founder of Client-Centered Therapy, who made the most notable impression.

He said, "If I can provide a certain type of relationship, the other person will discover within himself the capacity to use that relationship for growth and change—and personal development will occur."

Rogers saw his work, and the work of other psychologists, as the most important occupation in the world. In the long run, he believed that it was better interactions between people that would save us, not the physical sciences. He generated a climate of honesty and transparency in his sessions. If we simulated that environment in the family, in business, and in politics, Rogers felt there would be less anxiety in the world and positive outcomes.

Rogers' idea of creating a warm and candid atmosphere was my method of operation in my private practice, and in my consulting business. However, I combined many different approaches to therapy. Aaron Beck's *Cognitive Therapy* inspired much of my work. According to Beck, we constantly filter information and draw conclusions. This practice leads to inaccuracies, false beliefs, and negative emotions. He referred to cognitive distortions as patterns of faulty thinking. To change the way you behave, you must change your thought processes. Look for any declarations or judgments in your internal dialogue that make you feel hopeless or unhappy.

Once you and the therapist understand the thinking, you can fix the distortions that apply. All-or-nothing thinking is a distortion, thinking regarding absolutes and not recognizing the middle ground are misrepresentations. Jumping to conclusions and assuming the worst, even when there is not sufficient evidence to back that claim, is so often part of our inner discourse. These are just a few of the typical thinking patterns that we can change as we become aware of how these negative thoughts influence our behavior.

Most of my new patients had issues around anger. Many stood up, paced the room, and raised their voices. I frequently tried to get people to look at another problem because I was uncomfortable with their behavior.

The session couldn't be over fast enough to suit me. I began to doubt my ability to deal with angry patients. When people were docile and softly spoken, therapy was easier.

I realized that I had to deal with my anger first, or I wouldn't be able to successfully deal with fuming patients. I called my old therapist and found out that he retired and now lived in Israel.

I spoke with a colleague who gave me the name of a person he consulted. I started some serious work. I would have sworn that I didn't have much anger. I was pressured to confront the fact that even though I was content with my life at that juncture, I was also suppressing my anger.

This therapist was adept at dealing with psychologists like me and pushed me beyond my boiling point. This man would calmly say, "I think you're angrier than that. Show it. Yell, scream, do anything, but don't just sit there."

He wasn't the older male therapist that I previously had, or imagined. He was beyond handsome. Perfectly formed features, sky-blue eyes, prematurely gray hair, and a smile that told me how much he knew about women. His body quietly said, "I exercise every morning at 5 a.m. before I come to work." Dressed in khakis and a blue blazer, he created an instant image of *Shakespeare in Love*. I was intimidated and felt like a teenager.

"How are you ever going to let people show you how angry they are if you constantly deny the existence of your anger?" he asked me. "You will help them to conceal theirs rather than to face what is going on."

Often, I would end up in tears.

At some point during that year, it registered: I started to exhibit my true feelings. I was always the Pollyanna who tried to gloss over anything that created conflict. I typically went along with the consensus of my family.

For a while, I don't think I was very pleasant. I recall a specific event when my family wanted to adopt a fourth dog. A friend was moving to California. Her new apartment did not permit pets, and she had to find a new home for her year-old Golden Retriever. I did not want another animal in the house. "Fine" would have been my usual response. This time, I shouted with anger, "It's either the dog or me." My husband and children were shocked by my impulsive retort.

I was uncomfortable with my words and my actions, so I went back to see my therapist. Recognizing my feelings was important in the process, then I had options. I began to realize that I could be angry and chose whether or not to show it openly. I calmly talked through my anger or exhibited how I felt…not always a viable alternative.

I became more constructive when working with my patients. I helped people look at how things were, not just focus on how they thought they "should" be. "Should" statements are distortions. Eventually, I became popular as an anger management consultant and began to conduct workshops. Bloomfield and its neighbor West Hartford are small towns, and word-of-mouth brought in a dentist and his wife who had serious anger issues with in-laws. We worked together for several months, and they both learned to deal with their extended family peacefully, accepting their anger, but not always showing it. They kept their self-respect while coolly handling problems.

Simultaneously, the dentist had trouble with his office manager. This supervisor bullied the office. They wanted me to visit their place of business and see how unsuccessfully the manager handled the workers. Several of the people threatened to quit. After several office calls, I showed the manager what was happening to her staff. Things improved and this led to referrals for me to support other dental and medical practices. Here began the start of a consulting branch to my business. I no longer sat in my office all day, which was isolating. I worked in different settings with the staff of varied practices. I was recommended to work with small, family-owned businesses. I helped employees relate to one another more congenially and less competitively to eliminate as much friction as possible.

This division of my practice ultimately developed. I became relaxed with office managers, heirs and their in-laws, and all the anger they allowed themselves to exhibit. Each had a concept about how to do the work, and more time was spent trying to manage, rather than perform the job she was engaged to do. I knew that disputes wasted valuable time, and preserving the growth of the business and maintaining relationships with staff and clients was most important.

It became obvious to me that malfunction in the workplace corresponds to the difficulties in families.

People hide facts. Employees keep secrets. There are anxiety and trust issues. Relatives, as well as employees, are afraid to reveal what they honestly feel. There is a matriarch; it can be the mother and wife, one who comes to work every day, or an office manager taking on a similar role. She is usually the one who will be the catalyst for change. Once I understood the similarities, working with small companies or practices became as interesting and as challenging as working with families and couples.

Thanks to physician friends and a human resource person from a large insurance company, by the end of my first year in practice, I saw as many folks as my schedule permitted. I loved what I did.

14

"The Green Monster"

I wasn't a Shirley Temple lookalike, but I did have curly red hair, and I also started acting when I was a child. From the time I was four, I invented plays and performed all the parts to entertain my parents. The goal, although not clear to me at the time, was to take the focus away from their arguing. An argument could be as simple as what we were having for dinner. If Dad thought Mom changed her mind and decided to have something different, they would quarrel. If I diverted my parents' concentration to me, they forgot why they were angry with each other. It was work that I enjoyed. I had to think fast. They treasured the plays about *The Green Monster*, where I created another world for them.

I was the protagonist, a monstrous girl who looked like a tree, so I blended in with other trees and always had a refuge. I pretended I was an intimidating being and used a booming voice, gliding along the floor as gracefully as possible, using all the basic arm positions

I learned in ballet. I was determined to be as tall a tree as possible.

This tree, the way I portrayed her, was female. She had parents and two older brothers. Her family was all different versions of vegetation. This young "monster" had many tales of woe to share. Her room was tiny, so she slept on the beach. As the youngest, she was teased unmercifully by her siblings, and she found ways to seek revenge. She always knew the right thing to do, even when she broke the rules. She was brighter than most of her "tree mates," and often skipped school and went to the seaside. Her parents always found out because of something she slipped into conversation, although she knew that by telling them, she was headed for trouble.

Over the years, *The Green Monster* plays covered issues that pertained to my family, particularly matters that we never talked about: divorce, feelings, and manners. As I got older, I wrote many narratives in a notebook after I performed them. I was 10 years old when I staged these "productions." I still have some of the notebooks.

My parents encouraged my acting and my dancing. They enrolled me in drama and ballet classes in Manhattan when I was eleven. I rode the subway by myself. It seemed routine. My parents never doubted my safety, and neither did I. My dad didn't like to spend money on anything artistic, that was frivolous. Mom was delighted to see me involved in an activity outside of our home, particularly in the arts. My acting and dancing became important to my parents. They never complained.

I was in every play presented by my elementary,

junior, and high schools. When I was a teenager, drama was the most important activity in my life. The various schools I attended put on one production every year, until high school where there were several shows to choose from. I auditioned for a role in all the plays. I loved every bit of creating a new character on stage, and acting gave me a strong sense of myself.

When I was young, I performed the "story," and then I wrote it down. I didn't think about what I wrote, so it was simple. I quickly inscribed what I remembered, as I didn't want to forget a detail. Occasionally, I included the same storyline with a slightly different theme. My folks constantly argued. I needed all the fiction I could muster up.

As an adult, I spent a lot of my daughters' childhoods attending college and graduate school, but when I had the time, I shared *The Green Monster* tales with them. For my grandchildren, I made sure that they had as much of me as they wanted, including all my anecdotes. They cherished *The Green Monster* stories, just as my parents and daughters had before them.

Whenever the grandkids had a problem, the monster seemed to experience a similar problem, and always came up with a resolution – even if that explanation looked silly to the kids. During the year of the flashy Bar and Bat Mitzvahs, my oldest granddaughter was invited to most, but not all of them. When she was left out, she felt disappointed. Now it just so happened that Minerva, the green monster, occasionally wasn't invited to a party. To disguise her disappointment, she told her good friend that she despised parties. But the strategy backfired – because when that buddy threw a gala, she didn't invite Minerva. Angry and vengeful, Minerva decided to crash the party. Her friend was surprised but acted as if she had invited Minerva all along.

While both grandchildren thought Minerva was outrageous, they got a good laugh out of it, and it made rejection easier for them to tolerate. I always wished that my grandkids could've met Allan's version of "Dear Abby" through his Henries. The stuffed animals, with their altered voices, solved most of the etiquette and teenage problems that my children suffered through.

In the past few years, as an older adult, I returned to the freedom I felt in childhood. I can say pretty much anything in front of a group of people without being preoccupied by what they might think. But it will always be my reality to be careful, not to be foolish, or to hurt anyone's feelings. I'm experiencing a similar freedom with writing, and this craft has captured my full attention. I'm more open with what I put down on paper. I delight in the process of creating a story or a composition, and when I complete it to my liking, I'm content. It doesn't mean I don't struggle with every piece I produce. So, I can't say it is always fun, but it is almost always restorative.

It felt so easy to write when I acted out all the characters in *The Green Monster* stories. I acted out the improvised scripts; then I wrote them down. I was young. I didn't overthink them. They were entertaining. I used those tales to diminish my parents' conflicts and redirect their focus on something other than themselves. Now, it works the other way for me. Inscribing my stories helps me concentrate on myself, because at work and play, I often focus on others.

So, when I think of these tales and what they did for my folks, I realize their dysfunctional marriage helped me to be creative. I took a break from writing for many years, other than the papers I wrote to obtain my degrees. I'm back in the swing of things now, with a continued interest in handing down my chronicles to anyone interested in reading them. When I think of *The Green Monster* stories, those fabrications, and the role they played for my family, I relax, and they make me smile.

15

Allan's Heart Transplant

Allan's death was tragic.

Other than his heart functioning at 21 percent, he was in good health. At 65, he swam every day, his legs were strong, his weight hadn't fluctuated from 180 pounds in five years, and he was 5' 10". His liver and kidneys were working perfectly. His eating and drinking were never excessive. He still had his amazing light blonde hair, not a strand of gray, and large ocean-blue eyes. Skiing, both in Utah and in Stratton, Vermont where we had a vacation home, was one of his passions. The other one was golf. He played daily, weather permitting, and he won the "hole in one" award at his club that summer.

"Life is great," he would tell me and our daughters, Rachel and Janet. We were amazed at his positive attitude. We were also grateful for all he achieved in business. He became an expert at renovating and restoring buildings back to their original form. In his personal life, his daughters, sons-in-law and I adored him. He never raised his voice nor was he ever disapproving or judgmental.

He was attached to a defibrillator, a device for arresting fibrillation of the atrial muscles of the heart. This little machine beeped and delivered a dose of electrical energy to the heart if he went into dysrhythmia. Each time the machine made its piercing sound, the cardiologist needed to check it to ensure it was still working. That beeping sound also informed Allan that he would have died without it. With his optimism, he felt lucky to be alive. He was relentless in his pursuit of a healthy and long life. He was put on the transplant list and received the call that they had a match for him on January 27, 1997. This new heart was his vision for over six months, and he was the perfect candidate. It would enable him to have the time he needed to watch his grandchildren grow up, spend time with his family, and enjoy all his favorite hobbies.

Allan's vast coin collection was a hobby that completely consumed him. To find a Draped Bust Dollar coin that would round out his set, or the copper penny he needed because it completed his penny acquisitions, was a thrill. "Most wartime pennies are brass steel alloy, not the kind I want," he said. Because a dealer might not be aware of its authenticity, Allan didn't want the coin sent by mail. He'd book a flight to Long Beach, California, the site of the largest coin show in the country, to personally check out the coin himself. He always convinced me how important a particular coin was to his extensive collection.

Often, his need to leave at a moment's notice conflicted with previously made plans. After he was packed and almost out the door, he'd remind me to call friends with whom we had plans to rearrange the schedule. They were accustomed to his last-minute departures and changes in arrangements. Our friends and family understood that his need for these diversions kept him in the best of spirits. The frequent adjustments were not all that disappointing to me, and I never argued with him about all the plans I'd modified. Most of our commitments were business related. Socializing often revolved around Allan's country club cronies. The changes imposed were fine. I always found last-minute tickets to the Yale Repertory Theatre or Long Wharf Theatre, or I went to a movie. George often accompanied me. Allan always gave his blessings. It saved him from doing things he didn't particularly like. Allan treasured Broadway musicals, even the travelling shows that came to the Bushnell. He listened to the production recordings and sang every song from every show.

My one regret is that my career path prohibited me from travelling more with Allan, who longed for me to be a happy companion on all these jaunts. I, however, needed the satisfaction provided by a fulfilling and active career.

Allan called me on a Monday morning. I was at work with a crammed day ahead of me. He was elated. "They have the heart for me. Surgery is tomorrow morning. They want me at the hospital as soon as we can get there."

I quickly called my daughters, put a note on the door to my office, and drove downtown to pick up Allan. He seemed in a remarkably calm frame of mind, no different from the way he faced every challenge. We went to the emergency room at least five times during the prior month to manage Allan's heart failure. He stayed hospitalized for a few hours, loaded up on a new strength of a diuretic, then came home, dressed, and headed to work. If it were a weekend, he returned from the hospital, packed his gear, and went skiing in Vermont. At least one family member went with him to Vermont, but he was always ready to go alone.

Our small family walked into Hartford Hospital with Allan and met his transplant surgeon who was sneezing, coughing, and wheezing. "Doc, I am in better shape than you seem to be. Are you well enough to give me my new heart?" Allan joked. At that point, Janet and Rachel were my focus, and they looked horrified as the doctor kept blowing his nose.

Janet whispered, "How can he even consider operating on Dad? Look at how sick he is. This guy belongs in bed."

We stayed with Allan as long as we could. He was chatty and funny, as always. I was extremely anxious, broke out in a cold sweat, felt the butterflies in my stomach, and real fear for the first time. As we walked to the elevator, I started to cry. "What if he doesn't make it?" Rachel said. "I am not ready to lose him." Both girls got teary as well.

"With his heart functioning at 21 percent, he is in

constant heart failure, and probably won't live much longer anyhow. A heart transplant gives him a chance," I told them. The girls and I looked at each other and nodded.

Surgery appeared to go well. The doctor, who looked worse than the previous day, told us that the next few days would be critical. Allan was in intensive care and watched by the staff to see if he had signs of rejection. He had a few lucid and happy moments during the time that followed surgery. He had tubes in every part of his body. About the fourth day after the operation, he developed sepsis, a general invasion of the body by pathogenic microorganisms or their toxins. It was a horrible infection, and he went downhill very quickly. We'll never know, but we're all convinced that the doctor's illness gave him this abominable condition. We asked many physician friends about the surgeon's state of health as a possible cause for Allan's critical decline. They all agreed it was a distinct possibility.

Each day was more depressing than the one before. He underwent endoscopies, colonoscopies, blood transfusions, and MRIs. CAT scans were almost daily for two-and-a-half months. We wondered how many of these procedures were necessary. Several doctor friends hinted that the team of doctors might be keeping him alive to avoid our questioning about how he contracted this atrocious septicity. One of our family members was with him constantly. Allan was in so much pain that I prayed for his death. He died on April 14, 1997.

16

George

George was a brilliant man. Originally from Wisconsin, he was valedictorian of his high school class. He graduated from the California Institute of Technology and received his Ph.D. in Applied Mathematics from New York University, where he taught for some years. He was well-informed about astronomy, physics, literature, music, opera, and ballet. A professional cellest, he was also a gifted writer, and poet.

He spent many evenings and holidays at our home. There was no family in his life until we found his half-brother Hugo and his wife Penny on Facebook when George was in his 60's. We met them for dinner, and learned about Hugo's daughter, Lois, and her family. They were all musicians and lived in Massachusetts. Hugo was from George's dad's first marriage. He and his wife did not talk to George's family for 55 years.

George noticed beautiful sunsets and named all the planets and showed us where they were in the sky. At times, when he talked about the "black hole" and physics in greater detail than we all understood, we asked him to translate what he was saying.

Allan knew after he had two serious heart attacks that he might not make it to old age. He valued his free time and typically wanted to do what he liked. He understood my passion for the theater and the arts in general. George shared my interest in live theatrical productions, ballet, and opera. Since Allan only wanted to see musicals, he encouraged George to accompany me to any spectator event that he wasn't inclined to enjoy.

After Allan's death, our family home took two years to sell, and several years for me to adjust to Allan's absence. George was in the background with an offer to support in any way that he could. It did help with the loneliness and the loss. George eventually asked me to marry him, and although I cared about him deeply and we liked doing many of the same things, I thought it would complicate what we had together.

I decided to buy a house with George. That gave us time to see how we got along. We designed a place in a new over-55 community in West Hartford. It was a great move. We were compatible, and living together seemed natural. We never married, as I was afraid to change what worked so well.

We were fortunate to have my youngest daughter and her family close by, and my older child and her husband and daughters within two miles in the other direction.

George retired from his computer business at 60 and took great pleasure in writing music. His specialty at that time was electronic pieces using his computer. He performed his music at concert halls and universities all over the state…wherever he was invited.

He spent afternoons grocery shopping and preparing a gourmet meal for dinner. *The New York Times* crossword puzzle, done in ink, was completed in less than 20 minutes each morning.

In 2007, I had breast cancer. George wanted to share the experience with me at whatever level he could. He said it helped him to grow as a more compassionate person. He insisted on driving me to Saint Francis Hospital, five days a week, for several months, while I had radiation. Waiting in the hospital lobby or an ante-room, the doctors and technicians got to know him by name. It wasn't difficult for me to go alone. George said that being with me during that difficult time was essential and expanded his horizons. I couldn't say no to that kind of reasoning.

We saw my children and grandchildren often. If one of the girls needed a ride, George was available. If a dog needed walking, George was there with a leash in hand. I learned how to play Bridge with George; I never thought I'd surrender to adult games, but what I tolerated, I came to enjoy. We traveled once a year to Europe, and during the winter we spent time in a warmer climate.

We lived together for 12 years. George went to Saint Francis Hospital to have a mitral valve replacement and never woke up after surgery. Physicians at the hospital said that one person in a thousand dies after an operation of this kind. Devastation could not begin to describe my pain.

A memorial service for George was held in the theater at Real Art Ways in Hartford, not far from home. We have always been supporters of this coffee house, cinema for independent films, and gallery where local artists can exhibit their work. Will Wilkins, the director, knew George and respected his talent and lifetime support of this art space. Will introduced the evening and spoke about how honored he and his workers felt about having the commemorative service in their home. George was well-loved in the art community. He was a supporting actor or a reader, took out his cello when he was asked to play at a coffee house or to perform chamber music. He never said no if he was available.

My granddaughters led the service and both my daughters spoke eloquently about how George affected their lives. Emily, my oldest granddaughter, read an essay of George's. Peg, my youngest granddaughter read some of his poetry; Zoe introduced all the speakers. The theater was packed.

Rachel spoke about how George, along with her immediate family, was their dog Tommy's best friend, and how they will miss having him walk Tommy. She also spoke of how good he was to me. Janet told the audience that on the evening of George's death, "Venus appeared as a small dark dot crossing the sun's face for the last time this century. This event, called Venus' transit day, was the last transit of Venus in our lifetime. The brightest planet passed right in front of the sun for nearly seven hours on the evening of June 5, 2012. During the transit, Venus appeared to silhouette as a small, dark dot moving in front of the sun." She went on to say, "Why am I talking about this, I care little about Venus and the significance of June 5ᵗʰ as it relates to the planets. Most of you are here to learn more about George. For those of you who knew George, you were aware that he could talk endlessly about the planets, and frequently in greater depth and detail than what most people were concerned about hearing. It was his brilliance and passion that kept you riveted. We will all miss those conversations."

George's newly found niece and family from Massachusetts attended the service and played the cello and violin, portions of the chamber music that George greatly admired.

I sold the house shortly after George's death. It was too large. I needed to move on. I bought a place that was much smaller, but large enough for me to entertain family and friends. I thought that George would be around for a long time, entertaining the casserole crew after my death. One never knows.

17

Accepting What the Universe Creates

March 2007. George and I decided to escape the cold and rent a condo in Florida. This was the first time in 25 years that I took a month, all at once, away from work during the winter. Most psychologists, like myself, took the month of August to vacation. I always took at least that long. To make it a different experience, we chose the West Coast, Marco Island, just south of Naples. Prior trips to Florida were near family and friends on the East Coast. George wanted us to be less social and more relaxed. We spent a week in Naples during the previous summer, and we found a three-bedroom unit with a wraparound balcony in a newish Victorian-style building that faced the Gulf of Mexico. A similar place next door could be rented by the week and worked well for my oldest daughter, Janet, and granddaughters, Emily and Zoe, when the girls had their winter break from school.

Our place was lavishly furnished. Soft leather couches, Tiffany-style lamps, original modern paintings, and brocade drapery made a lovely first impression, but this unit was filthy and unorganized. It looked as if it had been rented to some young people who didn't care if the counters were sticky and the floors were sandy. The cleaners obviously didn't show up before we arrived. George and I hired two college students and worked with them to wash cabinets, appliances, bathrooms, and wooden floors. It took three days to get this condo clean enough and stocked with food so we could walk around without shoes, sit on furniture, enjoy our meals, and relax.

The fourth morning, we took a long walk on Tigertail Beach, half a mile away. We enjoyed breakfast at a diner across from our place, and strolled back to our condo to shower and dress for our friends Dee and Ed, who were driving from the East Coast to visit for the day. They spent winters in Florida. We saw them once a month when they came to Connecticut to check on their business.

As I was showering, I felt a lump in my breast. I was surprised, as I hadn't felt anything like that in a long time. Thirty years before, I had a similar inflammation, and although I knew they had fine physicians in Hartford, I chose to see a doctor who specialized in breast issues in New York City. It was a cyst and I had it aspirated. This happened a few times over the years, and I got to know the doctor quite well. He eventually retired.

I was lucky for many decades, so I was convinced this lump was breast cancer. What a downer, on the fourth day of a month-long holiday. I had a hard time thinking of anything else.

Should I tell George? He would want to take a plane to Hartford so I could see a doctor. *Do I call my primary care physician?* I know he would suggest seeing a specialist in Florida. *Perhaps I might make an appointment with a local doctor for an opinion?* I decided against all three options. Whatever it was would wait until we got back to Hartford on March 30th.

Over the next four weeks, instead of facing my problem, I diverted my focus onto other people, places, and things. I knew I was out of balance and couldn't find fulfillment in anything. It was hard to be present and find peace. Keeping this secret from George felt daunting. I didn't want to ruin the month we had planned. I thought I pulled it off. I'm sure I was deluding myself. George and I were conversational when we walked in the morning, or when we sat on our deck in the evening drinking a glass of wine. We were both unusually quiet. He thought I was tired of hearing people's stories and problems and needed meditative time. Acting had been my profession and avocation for so many years; pretending was second nature. The stakes of keeping this kind of secret were high. I compromised my ability to show up, be myself and speak the truth.

As the consummate actress, I thought I succeeded in showing my daughter and grandchildren a good time. We swam, picnicked, alternated our walk each morning on the two-quiet, pristine, public beaches, and ate in restaurants that had outdoor dining. Banana-grams and

Monopoly were daily pastimes, along with 1000-piece puzzles left on a side table until completed. I thought it might be therapeutic being with my family, but I had an underlying feeling of doom and sadness.

Enid visited for a few days and it was hard to keep my problem to myself. How could I tell her and not George? One moment I was writing my eulogy on scrap paper, thanking family and friends for putting up with my impetuous demeanor, and the next minute I was planning next year's vacation, but it wouldn't be here in Marco Island. Bad Karma. It was hard not to think about cancer and catastrophize.

My parents couldn't even say the word cancer. It was the "C" word. If you didn't call it by name then it didn't exist. I don't remember what they called the stomach cancer from which my grandmother died. My close childhood friend, Libby, passed away after complications from leukemia. What did they call her death?

The month ended and I didn't tell anyone. I phoned my physician a few days before we left Florida. His office made an appointment with a surgeon for a biopsy. I told George when we were seated on the plane going home. He was angry. I believe some of those feelings came from being excluded from something that was important to me.

"How could you keep this news to yourself? Didn't you trust that I could be there for you? How would you have felt if I didn't share something of this magnitude?" I knew that when George was frightened, anger was the first emotion that surfaced. I told him I was sorry and that

I didn't know how to handle it any better at the time.

Several days later, on a Wednesday, a general surgeon felt the now-prominent lump. He took a biopsy. He thought it might be a cyst, as the contents were liquid. I was hopeful. Friday, two days after my visit to his office, the doctor called and suggested an appointment to consult with him on Monday. Not a good sign. If all is well, you are informed by phone. You are only asked to come to the office when there is a problem. A weekend of angst was mixed with seeing family and friends. I did have George to talk to and that helped. *It doesn't have to be a death sentence*, I thought. I wanted to hear what the doctor said before I shared the news with my family.

Monday, I went into the office hopeful that it was a cyst. After waiting over an hour, I was called to sit down with the doctor. He looked at me and smiled, so I expected good news. He said, "Do you want the good news or the bad news first?"

"Whatever you feel comfortable with," I replied.

"It is indeed cancer, but I believe it might be self-contained. We won't know until you have surgery."

He suggested some further tests to evaluate. I told him I heard of a young woman who specialized in breast cancer. I read an article about her in the *Hartford Courant*. She had colon cancer and talked about her surgery in an interview. This person was going to be my surgeon. I made an appointment for the following week. I was impressed with this woman's knowledge and warmth. She suggested a battery of tests and an MRI. For anyone with claustrophobia, and I still had the remnants of an earlier disorder, this test was traumatic. For years, I sat in the aisle seat in the back of the theater at a movie or a play, so I could escape before feeling closed in by people leaving. I couldn't ride a subway until five years ago. I waited for someone to be in the elevator before I entered.

This particular machine was not only closed, but required me to lay face down. I hadn't taken tranquilizers in years. I asked the psychiatrist who prescribes medication to my patients to give me a prescription for Xanax. One wouldn't be adequate. I needed two .5 mg. tablets to get through that exam.

The test came back showing cancer in the other breast as well. It wasn't easily observed like the first. This one mass was deeper and not easily seen. I imagine I was fortunate to have found the first, more pronounced lump. This one wouldn't have surfaced until much later, and it might have been more serious. I also had two other suspicious spots that might have been benign. A double mastectomy seemed obvious. I was frightened about having cancer and also about losing both breasts. Further tests revealed one cancerous tumor in each breast along with benign tumors. I was relieved that a double lumpectomy was scheduled with lymph node biopsies instead of a double mastectomy.

It was the end of April, and since I was sure I had cancer since the beginning of March, it felt like forever. I scheduled to have surgery the second week in May. If my lymph nodes were clear it would be a one-day procedure. If there was node involvement, I would stay one night. Lymph nodes were tested in the operating room and were clear. I was told to relax for a few days and see my surgeon. Unfortunately, one breast had to have the surgery repeated as the margins were not clean. I was so thankful to have no lymph node participation that I almost considered myself fortunate to go back for another surgery.

George and my children waited while I had my surgery both times. A day after my second surgery, my two daughters and son-in-law came to visit. My younger daughter, Rachel, found a lump in her breast. After a biopsy and further tests, it was revealed that she also had bilateral breast cancer. It was advised that because of her young age, she have a double mastectomy. I was devastated. She was too young. It wasn't fair. I should have been the one having both breasts removed, not my 44-year-old child. She had a husband and a 10-year-old daughter.

This was a hard time in the lives of our family. With my husband Allan's death, there were only my two daughters and their small families. George was there for everyone, but no one could ever compete with Allan, their dad. He was larger-than-life to my children. My daughter went through surgery like a trooper, and fortunately, there was no lymph node involvement. No further treatment was needed. She did have to go through reconstruction and was sick for days from the anesthesia. Recuperation was not easy. She didn't complain. The trauma of losing both breasts and all the discomfort and drainage problems changed her life. She was calm and happy prior to this surgery. For the first time, I believe she experienced fear over the impermanence of her life. I was sad and frightened. I couldn't begin to express my feelings of helplessness.

I went through radiation for two and a half months, five days a week. No chemo. It was a short session, and then I returned to work. I had a busy practice, and being needed helped me to forget about myself and my child, at least temporarily. George insisted on driving me to the hospital every day and waited for me. He didn't accept no. He wanted to be as involved as possible. Other than fatigue, it wasn't difficult, but thinking about what my daughter went through was an unforgettable shock.

18

An Unforgettable
Round Trip

William Faulkner called Mark Twain "the father of American literature." Jane Austen was considered a literary icon, maybe even an English sister, so I guess George was labeled the "grandfather of electronic music." Not because I said so. George won first prize for his "Techniques for Programmed Electronic Music Synthesis" at the University of Paris – Sorbonne. He was awarded a cruise for two from New York to Southampton, England, on *The Queen Elizabeth 2*, with a return flight on the Concord. This astounded us. We never expected George to win this competition, no less first place. He wasn't going to enter his paper. Many of his more popular compositions went unnoticed and this less significant one was selected.

What would Jane Austen do with a trip comparable to George's prize in the 18th century? Austen lived a quiet life during her 41 years. Along with her writing, she embroidered and played the piano. She didn't travel. And what about Mark Twain? The country was still struggling internally over the matter of slavery, and most of Twain's adventures did not take place with Tom Sawyer and Huck Finn. He moved from city to city and was stimulated by steam boating. If Mark Twain could venture out to fascinating places in the 19th century – Mississippi, Nevada, California, Connecticut, and of course, Europe – we could certainly handle the five days it would take us to brave the waters on the *QE2*, cruising only one way. We would be flying back on a very fast plane. We liked boats and we were bold, but we truly disliked large cruise ships. We took the grandkids on a 3,000 passenger *Royal Caribbean* jaunt when they were young, and the voyage seemed all about Bingo, Trivial Pursuit, inferior entertainment, and islands that all looked alike.

I sound ungrateful, but five days without touching land, hmm, not so sure. I acted enthusiastic for George's sake, and because this voyage to England was the result of winning a prize, perhaps we would be greeted by a Duke and brought to the palace to have an audience with the Queen. George was a sailor, although he didn't like large ships either. How could we pass on this crossing? The trip was mostly free. We left in October 1999.

Characteristically, when we traveled, we liked being informal. From the chatter we heard from friends and family, the evenings on this ship would be rather "proper." They sent us first class all the way. That meant evening gowns and at least a dark suit for George, if not a tuxedo. He happened to have his dad's "monkey suit," and with some alterations and airing out (the moth ball smell was still pronounced), it would do.

We said our farewells to the family, who drove down to New York to see us set sail. In George's always romantic fashion, he ordered a bottle of fine champagne and opened it as the ship began its journey. We unpacked, turned on some lovely classical music, and dressed very formally for our first night in the first-class dining room. Giddy from the champagne and resigned to the trip, maybe even a bit excited, we found the beautifully appointed area called "Chez George." The restaurant was more than striking. Chandeliers hung from the ceiling that reminded us of a Jahoolie work of art (the artist who does everything in glass), soft velvet chairs, tables with five-stemmed glasses at each place setting, and dazzling Limoges china. A small group of musicians played Bach, Mozart, and Mendelssohn, which bolstered our mood. We were pampered by staff, including the waiters dressed in tuxedoes who spoke with British accents.

Something was missing. A few minutes after dinner was served, we noticed that we and another couple, also seated at a table for two, were the only people in the dining room. It was October and slightly off season for a transatlantic cruise. The waters could get rough and the ship was a little shaky. George and I were used to harsh waters; even though I am not a good swimmer, we loved the sea, and usually didn't get seasick. Along with the waitstaff, the four of us had the dining room to ourselves.

I said, "George, If Jane Austin was convinced to cruise

on this ship, don't you think she would have been in her room, frightened and crouched in the corner of her bed, trying to embroider a tablecloth? Mark Twain would have started the evening at a table for one, but after a cocktail or two, he would have asked to join us, talking about the calamities on his many boat excursions. The other couple and the waiters would have been part of his audience, and of course he would be entertaining."

We enjoyed our dinner and decided to explore the ship. We visited the casino, and other than the dealers, it was empty. We located the fitness center and the library and didn't meet a person along the way. This large ship a ghost town!

The next day, a few people ventured out of their cabins. Many guests were queasy as the ocean was still intense. George and I enjoyed having the space to move around. We ventured into the shops, said "hello" to the Captain, and dropped in on lectures about England's history. By the third day, as the old Greek adage goes, "Fish and guests in three days are stale." The ship needed some sprucing up. The main rooms were getting sloppy. Trash bins needed emptying, dirty glasses were everywhere, and people had been ill, obviously, as there was an unpleasant aroma in many of the areas. We were restless and couldn't wait to touch land. We returned to our suite after dinner to read. We were tired of the entertainment, the casino, and staying up too late. After the first night, the food was not very good. We were worn out. Supposedly a restful vacation and yet we didn't feel rested.

We probably dozed off at around 11:00 p.m. At midnight, the phone rang. We were both in a deep sleep. I quickly answered and the voice on the other end said, "This is an emergency. We are going to have some rough weather. Please proceed down the back staircase to the hospital and get some Dramamine." I grew panicky. I started to dress, and George called the switchboard to learn some additional information. The man at the other end of my alarming phone call hung up abruptly. The woman at the telephone exchange had no idea what was going on and said, "I will speak to the Captain and let you know what is happening." A few minutes later, what felt more like an hour, the phone rang and the woman said, "The weather hasn't changed and they have no idea who called us." I couldn't go back to sleep. I was anxious and stayed up all night trying to read.

The next morning, we found out that ten cabins received the same phone call. It was a hoax. One more day. I couldn't wait to exit the ship. Somehow the phone call brought up all kinds of "what ifs" for me. Mainly, I thought of the Titanic. The next night I still couldn't sleep. By the time we left the luxurious cruiser, I was exhausted. There was no Duke or anyone else to greet us when we docked. I was only slightly disappointed, mostly relieved that it was just the two of us; I had a terrible cold.

We spent a week at the Ritz in London. My favorite city looked dismal because I felt sick. I eventually saw a physician. What started out as a cold became bronchitis. I couldn't stop coughing. Our trips to London usually meant a marathon theater week. We managed to see two shows in one day, each day, most of the week. George and I loved sitting in the first few rows of the orchestra. After the first day, and a coughing fit, with all eyes on me from the spectators as well as the cast, we decided we would sit in the last row for future plays, on the aisle, so I could make a mad dash for the exit when I started coughing. I felt demanding. A free trip and all I could think about was going home. One play blended into the next. I couldn't even remember what we saw. The week dragged by and I was cranky. I finally felt better the day before we were slated to fly home.

At 8:30 the next morning, we arrived at the British Air Terminal where the Concord was to depart for a 10:00 a.m. flight. We were treated like celebrities. A gentleman took our baggage as soon as we arrived. We were handed Mimosas and escorted into a lovely room where breakfast was served. White cloths were on the tables along with a complete silver service and handsomely attired waiters. I was enthusiastic. Not only were we going home after a less than mediocre trip, but we were leaving in style. At 9:30 we were told that we were boarding. We finished our coffee and walked down the passageway to the plane. We walked to the door of the cabin, looked in, and I said to George in my claustrophobic fashion, "There is no way I can do this. I am not stepping foot into this tube that they call a plane."

I was panic stricken and was not moving into that small space. George called the flight attendant over and said, "My wife is having trouble entering this narrow compartment, would you please remove our baggage? We'll find another British Air flight home."

The attendant was definitely thrown and said, "Please do not make us take off your luggage. We cannot fly with baggage unless the passengers are on the plane. This interruption will affect the time we leave."

"I cannot do this," I said. I was terrified and it was obvious.

"You're not the only one who has felt this way," the attendant said. That remark was meant to be helpful. "We've had many people leave before takeoff. Please let me convince you to fly with us. Once seated you will not mind at all. I will also throw in two bottles of Dom Perignon to have you stay."

How little it takes to turn my head around. I also felt guilty in delaying the flight. I succumbed to the pressure and said with a smile, "I'll try." I walked in, shaking, and sat down. George followed, quite relieved, hoping I could stay seated. Two people behind us were producers of a movie they were filming in Waterbury, Connecticut. They leaned over and said that they went through the same anxiety the first time they flew the Concord. This was a delightful couple who chatted with us as the plane left the runway and most of the way home. I felt better and began to relax. I cultivated a real taste for flying, but this was a new and distinct experience. I wanted to land, and luckily it took only a little more than three hours to arrive at New York's Kennedy Airport. I forgot about my bribe, but as we left, the steward thanked us for staying on the plane and handed me two beautiful wooden boxes of champagne.

We were happy to be back in the States. Only a two-hour drive until we reached home. We unpacked, and after chilling one of the bottles of champagne, uncorked it, poured it into our fine crystal glasses, and George made a toast. "To us, and to the trip that has inspired us to stay home for a while."

19

Flip Flop Fiasco

It was early Saturday afternoon. George was doing his crossword puzzle and eating a grilled cheese and tomato sandwich. He was listening to a CD of Bartok at the piano, waiting for me to get ready to go to a four o'clock movie. I was catching up on paperwork and an insurance report before leaving for London with Rachel the following Saturday to celebrate her 50th birthday. Being the compulsive person I am, I decided to take a pair of rubber flip flops with me. I don't like walking without shoes in hotel rooms. "Where did I leave my flip flops?" I asked George. I looked all over the house but couldn't find them.

My office phone rang. It was unusual for me to receive calls on a Saturday. I picked up the phone and heard a frantic voice on the other end. "Dr. Schaefer, is there a possibility that you might see me this afternoon?" She started to cry hysterically. "Peter just asked me for a divorce and told me that he no longer has feelings for me. He's in love with his secretary. What do I tell my children?" she asked me, while sobbing. "Please can you see me this afternoon?"

I looked at George with pleading eyes. George, who sat at the kitchen counter, shook his head yes. "I can see you in an hour," I said.

When I saw patients in my upstairs office, George went downstairs to his office or studio where he composed music. He finished his lunch and before he disappeared, he turned the music off in the dining room and said, "I think your flip flops are behind the drapes in front of the deck." They were. I took them into the laundry room and put them in the sink, added kitchen soap and started running water on them. I also used the shoes outside, in the garage, and when I painted. They were colorful, but very dirty.

The doorbell rang. Most people don't come by without calling. My daughter and her family live three houses away, but they always call. Maybe Peg was home from school and wanted to surprise us. I opened the door and there was my patient, Liz. "I know I'm early. I had to take my daughter to a soccer game and I was so close. I hope you don't mind." She looked so anxious that I said, "Of course, come in." I led her into my office and we both sat down. She found some receipts in her husband's jacket pocket from a nearby hotel. (She always checked his pockets on the way to the cleaners.) She went to New York for business several days that week, and the dates corresponded with the time she was away. When she saw the hotel receipts, she confronted her husband. He was tongue tied. She had a tantrum and threw herself on the floor and remained there screaming until he finally admitted the truth.

She was suspicious of her husband, who was usually very sexual. He hadn't wanted to be intimate with her for months. "But he was so nice to me," she said. "That is when I became more mistrustful, because, up until then, he had been mean to me." Her children came home from school one afternoon and didn't see Peter's parents in the living room. They went to their rooms and never acknowledged their grandparents, but Liz didn't call the children down to say hello.

"They told me that I was spoiling my children and that they were brats," Liz said. "What an awful thing to say. I asked Peter's parents to leave." All hell broke loose, and his parents refused to come back to the house, even to celebrate their granddaughter Victoria's birthday. Peter was furious with Liz.

"Suddenly, Peter was nice to me again; that's when I found the hotel bills." He admitted that he was having an affair with his secretary and thought he wanted to leave the marriage. The tears were flowing freely as Liz asked, once again, "What will I tell the children?" The session ended and we made an appointment for the following Friday, a day before my trip to London.

It was too late to go to the 4:00 movie. I considered a 7:00 movie and an early dinner. I went to the laundry room to put some clothes in the washing machine. OH MY GOD! I was ankle deep in water. My flip flop became a sink stopper. The water was still running and was five inches deep in the laundry room, in the garage, the back hallway, and leaked downstairs to George's office and bathroom. George must have been in his studio. I ran to the linen closet and pulled out a load of towels and yelled for George, who sprinted up the stairs two at a time. I was crying and apologized for being so careless. George reassured me by saying "It's okay. It was an accident, these things happen." He never made me feel bad. He blamed my client for coming early and distracting me. I was never at fault in George's eyes.

We were in trouble. All the towels in the linen closet couldn't begin to mop up 50 minutes of running water. The house was a mess. We were concerned about mold and damage to the walls. The office downstairs, where George had his computers and some of his electronic musical instruments, was soaked. We had to call for help. We looked in the yellow pages and found a company called Service Mister. They had fans and wet vacuums, and for a steep price, they would arrive in 30 minutes.

Service Mister showed up on schedule with four people, three fans, and several vacuums to catch all the water. The company asked if we had insurance. Of course, what homeowner doesn't? They thought it would be important to contact our insurance agent on Monday because the damages exceeded $30,000. We needed someone to replace sheetrock, draperies, flooring and God only knew what else. I was a little concerned, as I lost a diamond earring in Saint Bart's a few months before and collected for it. How would our insurance company react to another claim?

The mess was unbelievable. The sheetrock in George's office needed to be replaced. The bathroom paper was peeling off the walls. Our beautiful home was in shambles, and it was my fault. The week before, eggs exploded in the kitchen area because I walked into our bedroom and the water boiled out of the pot. While George cleaned the eggs off the ceiling, I promised never to leave a room if something was cooking. I also vowed to never leave water running unless I was in the room. Look what I did. I was the compulsive person in the couple. George's office looked like a tornado had hit, but didn't compare to the disaster I created.

I thought of cancelling my trip. George wouldn't hear of it. He handled all the necessary details to get the house back in shape. He also dealt with the insurance company. They paid the claim, but they dropped us. Our agent earned her hefty fee, as she had trouble finding a company comparable to the one we previously had. What was so reaffirming was how George maintained love and respect for me. Friendship kindles romance, but also guards against a relationship getting combative. We maintained that friendship, affection, and appreciation. My reverence for George was never as great.

20

Death Is Around the Corner

It was 8:00 a.m. on a perfect summer day in 2010. My son-in-law Victor and his dog Oliver walked out to retrieve yesterday's mail. Victor spent most of his time alone, with Oliver, while his daughter Peg, a child actress, was in a show. My daughter Rachel traveled with her. Peg was in *Les Misérables* for 18 months. Victor traveled on weekends to be with them. A friend came to stay with their dog. The kennel was not good enough for Oliver. Cramming his work into 12-hour days, three times a week, Victor met Rachel and Peg in California or Arizona, anyplace where there was a performance.

During the week, George and I received texts from Victor, usually around 6:00 p.m. "The Bar is Open," they read, and we walked past the three houses which separated our homes to share a bottle of wine with him. Victor often invited us to stay for dinner. His cuisine far surpassed ours. It didn't matter if I prepared a roast beef and it was in the oven cooking; we ate it the next day, or we put it in the freezer. Spending time with Victor was important to us.

Victor came from Romania, a communist country, and he was a man of few words. When we got him talking, he rewound his experiences, and revived some of the highlights with an endless string of tales about the role of government, and life there in general. As he looked at his circumstances, he had pride and self-respect. He described waiting in line with his folks many hours, for a few gallons of gas. The regime rationed food and paper goods. His family and most of his neighbors grew their produce and raised chickens and goats while working full time in a shop or a manufacturing plant. Some members of his clan worked for the secret police. Many people in his family were professionals, now forced to do menial work. Bugging the tables in restaurants was common practice by the government. People were always careful about what they said.

We chatted with him about politics or theater, or our day-to-day happenings. I saw clients at home, and George composed music. We always had something to share with Victor. He was always interested.

We also learned to enjoy silence with Victor and fill that soundless space with soothing thoughts. In a world of perpetual uproar, stillness became therapeutic.

Victor was as caring and helpful to us as he was to his wife, Rachel, and daughter, Peg. We called him if we had a problem with a crashed computer or a garage door that wouldn't open. He fixed most anything, however hard the challenge.

George was Oliver's backup, and he became Oliver's dog walker, dog feeder, and his grandfather. But Victor's alone time with Oliver was special. They had an unusual way of communicating. Oliver followed Victor from room to room and would bark in a definite way. Victor answered him in his commanding but quiet manner, and we were sure, as observers, that they knew what the other was thinking. Rachel had breast cancer when they bought this amazing mixture of King Charles and Cocker Spaniel. She wanted a dog, they all did, for several years, since moving to their new house.

Rachel and Victor relocated from England to live with us and help with the family real estate business. We offered them a private three-room apartment in our house where they enjoyed the wide-ranging property. We happily lived together for eleven years. They brought their King Charles spaniel to join our three dogs. We had two King Charles Spaniels and a Springer Spaniel. They were close in age, and within several years, they all died.

That summer, Peg was in *Radio Girls* at the Goodspeed Opera House in East Haddam, Connecticut, so she and Rachel stayed in Haddam. George developed a heart issue and was in the hospital for a week. I stayed with Victor during that time to help with the dog and keep him company. Victor kept me sane. George's heart problem was difficult for me. It came as a shock to both of us. He was in great shape. He exercised an hour a day, ate healthy food, and had good genes. He had a mitral valve problem. It was a matter of time before he needed surgery. It took two years.

Oliver and I walked for an hour in the morning, at a fast pace, and I took him for a stroll after I finished seeing clients while Victor cooked dinner.

That summer morning, as Victor and Oliver retrieved their mail, I was in my home office, working. I had dinner plans with friends that evening. When I arrived at Victor's at 8:30 p.m., I was confronted by a person I didn't know. Usually cool, confident, and patient, Victor was shaking and crying hysterically. He could barely get the words out.

"Oliver is dead. A neighbor killed him, and she never stopped driving."

He described the car and the person. I knew who she was. Oliver stopped for a moment to contemplate a piece of wood before joining Victor, and the woman ran over him. Victor had some work done at the house and she was looking at the new construction instead of paying attention to her driving. The workmen saw what happened and were shocked that she kept moving. Victor picked up the dog and had one of the workers drive him to the veterinarian's office. Oliver died on the way.

Rachel and Peg were coming home for a few days. Victor was panicked. "How can I tell them?" It was a difficult scene to witness. Rachel was beyond distraught. I never saw my daughter in such excruciating emotional pain.

They had to confront this driver, Fran; she knew what happened. Her garage door, usually open, was closed for the entire weekend.

I asked Rachel and Victor to get in touch with Fran's daughter. The woman was elderly, and I was afraid that she might have a heart attack when confronted. Her daughter showed up at Rachel's house shortly after the call. Instead of apologizing, which might have occurred on the day of the accident, Fran said she didn't know that she ran over the dog. We couldn't argue, but we all knew that she was aware. Never a letter of apology or any sign of remorse. She told another neighbor that she was afraid of being sued. Just as a dog can magnify your life, broaden your focus, and bring you unqualified love, a woman like our neighbor can make you cynical, bitter, and vengeful. I only hoped that Rachel, Victor, and Peg could find it in their hearts to forgive her…for their sake. They still refer to her as the "Dog Killer."

She ultimately moved.

Shortly after this incident, Victor, Rachel, and Peg adopted Tommy, a ruby red King Charles Spaniel, who is currently 9 years old and is a joy to the entire family.

21

Moving On

I had a thriving practice and felt a responsibility to my patients. I likewise had the travel bug. Balancing my life was always a challenge for me. I could not in all good conscience take more than a month off during the summer and a few weeks in the winter. We traveled as a family when we had time. Our children visited far-off places with Allan when I wasn't available. Allan and my brother Yale were not only in business together, but they were best friends and often went skiing together when family members weren't available. They both loved that sport.

During the mid-1980s, Rachel graduated from Boston College, and Janet earned her Master's at The University of Connecticut, after receiving her undergraduate degree from The College of the Holy Cross. They came home often. Rachel was a Linguistics major. She realized that she could travel all over the world, speaking different languages if she studied them. Her interest suited all members of the family, as we enjoyed having her translate for us when we journeyed. Romanian was her choice in her senior year. She took all the other Romance languages. She spent a few months in Romania when life was tough for the people living there and cherished the experience. After getting a Master's in Communications, Rachel moved to London to work for Italian television. She met her husband Victor at a Romanian church function; he was from Romania and had defected, he came for a business meeting and never went back.

Janet had many interests around medicine and health but decided to major in finance to help Allan if he needed her assistance. She moved to Cromwell after graduation and worked for Aetna, where she met her husband Michael who was from Poland. It is interesting that two privileged, charming, but somewhat indulged young ladies married Eastern European men who came from Communist countries. Janet changed careers and became a diabetic educator and a nutritionist, closer to the medical field.

My brother Don died when the girls were in school, and it made me angry and sad. He was poorly diagnosed. He and his wife were hippies. They lived on a commune in Mendocino County, California. They were Socialists and lived a different lifestyle than my oldest brother, Yale, or my family. They were minimalists before it became trendy. My brother went to a holistic medical person for a stomach ailment. The doctor treated him for an ulcer. He had cancer. It was too late by the time they figured out what was wrong with him. When he died at 47, he left Muni, his six-year-old son and Anneka, his three-year-old daughter. They have always been my other children, although they have a good mother.

Allan and I made beautiful weddings for both daughters. Rachel and Victor married in 1989 and moved back to Bloomfield from London to help with the real estate business in the early 1990s, as Allan was sick. We had a large enough house to make an apartment for them so they could have their privacy. They still work successfully in real estate.

Janet and Michael married in 1992 and moved to West Hartford. Both couples have daughters; Janet and Michael have Emily and Zoe, and Rachel and Victor have Peg. Allan got to see them all, but died when Emily was three, Zoe was a year, and Peg was seven months. What a disappointment that he couldn't get to see the success of his children and grandchildren! Peg was a professional Broadway actress at eight years old. She was in *Les Misérables*, traveling all over the country with her mom, and she was in *Billy Elliot* on Broadway for almost two years. She was in the next-to-last movie that James Gandolfini starred in before he died, *Not Fade Away*. Peg acts, dances, and sings beautifully to the genre of music that Allan loved, songs from Broadway musicals.

Emily and Zoe are athletes. They played soccer and squash with JV and varsity teams, and they also ran track. Zoe took to lacrosse. They all ski, and Emily and Zoe play golf. What fun would they have had to bond with Allan, sharing the activities they all value? The girls are good students. Emily graduated from Colgate University and works in New York City. Zoe graduated from Trinity

College in Hartford, Allan's dad's alma mater, and also works in New York. Peg graduated from Yale in 2019. We were lucky to have Allan for as long as we did. He lived 24 years after a massive coronary, but not long enough.

I was fortunate to have George in my life after Allan died. We lived happily for 12 years until he passed away. Five years ago, on September 6, 2012, two months after George died, I sold the house we shared and moved into my condo. I had two months to move out of my house. It sold in one week, with all the furnishings. My son-in-law Victor came with me to look at several units before I chose my current one. I kept my clothing, my kitchen accessories and my artwork.

My new condo is three times smaller than my previous home. As I was moving in, I said to my daughter, Rachel, "How can I possibly fit my things into this place?"

She replied, "Well, you start by giving away all but what you treasure."

I did just that. It was cleansing. I have what I wear, not what I might wear. Do I need three sets of China? I don't think so. I entertain infrequently; my everyday Wedgewood is fine. Four pots and pans are sufficient. I will never use them at the same time. If something didn't fit in one of the cabinets, it found a new home.

I decided that the Heritage at Blue Back Square in West Hartford was the only place for me to live. According to Wikipedia, "Blue Back Square was built in 2008 and named after Noah Webster a West Hartford resident, and author, who wrote *The Blueback Speller*.

American children read this book for five generations. Blue Back Square has grown to be a popular hub of activity for locals and out-of-towners, filled with great shopping, dining, and entertainment."

I like the idea of a small building near the square, with a gym, and apartment-type units that are all unique. A ten-year-old building, it has two spacious community rooms, one with a fireplace, couches, and bookcases, and the other room with a full kitchen and dining room. I can reserve either community room for meetings, workshops, my writing groups, and parties. A gated parking area makes the building safe, and more than anything, I need to feel secure.

The day I first saw the condo, I walked from room to room and couldn't believe that a stunning flat like this would be in West Hartford. I felt a divine connection. It was perfect, and yet I was teary and thought that George should be moving in with me. I not only wanted George back; I wanted my husband Allan back. I would have also accepted any of my previous boyfriends back. I couldn't fathom living alone, and it would be challenging. As brave as I thought I was, I was holding on tight, and couldn't have moved without the immeasurable help from my family and friends.

The price was as steep as the house I sold. It wasn't on the market, yet. I knew I was the first potential buyer to see this place, and if I didn't give the agent a deposit, someone else would. I visualized myself living there. It reminded me of a small New York City apartment, nicer than the one in which I grew up. The turnover in this building is sporadic, and I didn't want to move out of my house without a permanent place to go, but I was hesitant and indecisive. With encouragement from my son-in-law Victor, I decided to buy it.

My condo is on the second floor, above a furniture store, on the northeast corner of the building. There is a small foyer, big enough for a table and mirror. The living space is large, bright and open. The kitchen, dining, and living room are one, just like my old house. Windows are on three sides, and a small French-style balcony faces Crate and Barrel and two busy streets. Each room has an impressive contemporary glass chandelier that captures light and space. They look as if they belong in an elaborate hotel. I am a crystal enthusiast, so the chandeliers are especially appealing. When I first married, I visited all the second-hand junk shops and bought one cut glass candleholder. I couldn't afford the pair. I eventually collected over 300 odd pieces. As I downsized, I gave most of them away. The fixture in my office is hand blown, in amber, gold, and clear glass. The living/dining room has a sculpture on the ceiling in the shape of icicles, not traditional and not modern. The bedroom fixture is boudoir type, large and multi-tiered pure glass.

Two lovely trees frame the large picture window. A master bedroom and bath are on one side of the unit. A second bedroom and a bath, on the other end, could serve as an office or an extra bedroom if I needed it for guests.

I bought new, contemporary furniture that suits this modern condominium. I am pleased with my choice of a home, particularly because I live alone. There are people around if I want company, but folks are private here. I don't have any pressure to interact. My next door neighbor, who moved to Arizona, was a delightful gentleman and became a helpful friend. He was supportive when I first settled here. He often reminded me that it was cocktail time, someplace, and I had to join him. He didn't like drinking alone.

For a while, I played a weekly game of Bridge in the community room. I started going to the gym and still do. I always walk around the center and do my shopping at Whole Foods, also in walking distance. Friends come for drinks before going to various restaurants. A handyman is on the premises to change lightbulbs, heating and air filters. He does all kinds of odd jobs. We also have a concierge.

It is delightful to live close to my children. If I don't walk to dinner, I can often wangle an invitation to one of their homes for a superb meal. They have a good cook in each of their families.

For a year and a half, this condo even became large enough for two. Once again, I did a massive giveaway. If I bought a new item, something was donated. I no longer visited shops, except to buy consumables.

This condo is serene and peaceful. It is my dreamscape, my castle, and it is now home.

22

Yuko

George was the one in a thousand who died from a mitral valve replacement during surgery. We said goodbye that morning. I walked with the nurse and technician as they wheeled George into the operating room. I told him about the things we would do while he recuperated: *Downton Abby* episodes we taped and didn't have time to watch, meals he taught me to cook that I would try to reinvent, the music he composed and put on videos that we would watch all in one sitting. My children and grandchildren would visit and listen to his stories, I told George with a smile.

It was June 5, 2012.

A month later, I decided to tell Zhi Chin and Kumio, owners of one of our most frequented local restaurants, about George's sudden death. We had just been there a few nights before George went in for surgery, and we ate at least three meals a week at this Chinese/Japanese establishment, a little over a mile down the road, for most of the 11 years we lived together.

I asked my friend Enid to have dinner with me that Monday evening. It was a few days after George's Memorial Service. I knew I would break down and cry and didn't want to be alone. Enid was amenable. Sure enough, I walked in the door, and saw Zhi Chin and started sobbing. Zhi Chin and her husband had become our friends; we, along with their staff, and many family members who were in the area, had celebrated the Chinese New Year with them on each of the previous few years. We became part of their family. We were often in the restaurant during one of their crises, the death of Kumio's twin brother in Japan, and Zhi Chin's father in China. We had dinner with them the night I learned of my breast cancer, and again a month later after my surgery when I learned that my daughter Rachel also had breast cancer. Our traumas, as they occurred, were usually more palatable while eating their salt and pepper shrimp or their freshly carved salmon sashimi.

Zhi Chin started to cry as soon as she saw me. I wasn't with George, I was hysterical, and she knew something catastrophic had happened. Sharon, their loyal and longtime server/hostess, also close to us, ran over and started to weep as well. I hadn't even told them that George died.

I didn't have to order. May, one of our usual waitpersons, brought me and Enid my customary glass of Cabernet, and shortly after, my favorite shrimp dish and assorted freshly carved sashimi. Zhi Chin and Sharon sat down with us and asked what happened. Because I had trouble regaining my composure, I became the focus of many eyes in the restaurant. Usually, that kind of attention would bother me, but that night, I didn't care.

"How can we help?" they asked. A 4000-square-foot home was too large for me as a newly single woman, but downsizing was overwhelming and so was the idea of living alone for the first time.

I had to move in two months. George was a hoarder of sorts who had all his parents' stuff plus his own. A musician, he had accumulated 12 musical instruments. I knew that he'd want me to give many of his possessions to colleagues and friends. His prized cello went to a close friend's son, who was also a cellist. My children worked with me to sort through belongings, and so did my grandchildren. I certainly didn't want to be a burden, nor did I want to ask them to help me on the weekends when they finally had free time.

Zhi Chin started smiling when I explained my needs, and she suggested that I meet her daughter, Yuko, who, she believed, would be more than willing to help me. I saw a glimmer of hope. I never thought I would ever finish packing. I never dreamed that I could give away George's belongings to the appropriate people by August 30th. Impossible.

"Yuko and her boyfriend just broke up, so helping you will keep her busy in the evenings after her work hours when she usually spent time with that guy. It would be good for her to meet you and maybe you can help her figure out why she chooses men who don't appreciate her," Zhi Chin told me.

Shortly after I got home, Yuko phoned and we made plans to meet the next day. She rang the doorbell the next evening, promptly at 5:30, right after work. I asked her if she had time for dinner, as her mom told me that she got out of work at 5:00 p.m. She said that she had a protein bar with her and it would suffice. I suggested that we go out for dinner and get acquainted. She agreed and we went to Max Burger, a local place, not her parents' restaurant. We had salads and talked for several hours. I explained what I needed, and we decided on an hourly rate. We didn't work that evening.

I was fond of this beautiful woman from the moment I saw her. She has long shiny black hair, often worn in a high ponytail. She is tall and thin and has the knack of putting together a fashionable wardrobe on a slim bud-get. She always looks trendy. Her infectious smile high-lights two dimples that could captivate the grouchiest of folks. It takes a great deal to get Yuko ruffled, as her manner is easy-going. Although not always as resilient as she appears, she is cool and calm in most situations. She became my friend, confidant, and surrogate daughter, young enough at 29 to be a granddaughter. She became someone I could count on to help me with the computer, for she is a whiz. Incredibly neat and tidy, she solved my packing and storage issues, and during income tax time, she handled all of my accounting problems and made them look simple.

Because of Yuko, I made my target moving date. We worked together to gather George's belongings and pack mine. Although he didn't have anyone close, George did have some distant family members who were as musical as he, people who would enjoy receiving some of his instruments, and other folks who would cherish his family photos and movies. His dad carefully described their camping trips in 25 lengthy journals, each one the size of a world atlas. I shipped these books to his only living half-niece and her family. Of course, his second cousins wanted some of George's dad's blueprints. His dad was an architect who designed hundreds of churches in Wisconsin. The house that the cousins lived in was designed and built by George's dad and it was left to George, who gifted it to his cousins.

While I was moving, I paid Yuko for all the work she did for me. Gradually, as we became good friends, she didn't want to take any money. We spent many evenings together. We worked on projects, like making lavender oil, and we went from store to craft shop just to find the right spray container. She joined my family on Christmas Eve and many other evenings. She listened to my dating tales, and I listened to hers. She introduced me to her boyfriends, and I hosted them for dinner to check them out. Yuko got to know my boyfriends and always had a positive remark to share.

At the time, Yuko had been working at the same job for the last five years, a position in a marketing company that paid her much less than she was worth, and where she was not shown the respect someone with her many skills and talents deserved. She started a master's program in business when we met. We talked about a change in careers when she finished the program. She took her last course in September 2014 and completed all the degree requirements that December. She looked for a position in this area but wasn't successful in finding something that would pay her enough to move out of her parents' home and eventually buy a place of her own. She had an opportunity to interview with the Ford Company in Michigan and went there for the experience. Not surprising to me, but a complete shock to Yuko, she was offered a well-paid position with the Ford Company in Atlanta. She continued to search for something that would be financially rewarding in the Hartford area. No success. She decided to take the job, along with the car she would receive after training, and the adequate moving expense money. She would gain some independent experience.

I was happy for her, as the lifestyle change from living at home with parents, as well as a new livelihood in a different city, would be a period of growth for her. She left for China, before starting her new position, for a celebration of her grandfather's 100th birthday, although it was posthumous. She left for three weeks. She was home for one day and then off on her own.

The night before Yuko went to China, she had dinner with me, and I cried as I wrote this last paragraph, as I did unexpectedly as we hugged goodbye. The tears started streaming down my face, and once again, I was sobbing. She has been the most wonderful, caring, and loving friend. I do not feel any age difference. I feel young when I am with her, and we laugh a lot. She is very wise. I learned many life lessons from this young woman, and I am a psychologist. She pauses when agitated, and she almost always gives the other person the benefit of the doubt. She could have written the *Mastery of Love*. We kept closely in touch, but I missed the day-to-day contact we had. I will always be grateful for our friendship and her love.

Yuko met a lovely man before she moved to Atlanta, and after spending almost two years down south, her company found a position for her in Connecticut. I believe I am as thankful as her man friend and her folks that she is back in this area. Our friendship continued, and she is still a big part of my life.

23

Dating Disaster

You can see me online. I was on television and in four newspapers in the Hartford area. Simply look up "Senior Woman, 75 years of age, sues Dating Service." The story cites my name, my occupation, that I am from West Hartford, and that I've had two husbands who are both deceased. People probably thought I was courageous or desperate to consider meeting strange men through a business. One catering to oldies? Well neither can I. Women will usually meet men through friends. I tried that. Most of the men I met through people were not for me. The few that I met were too old, both in body and in attitude. How foolhardy can a widow of any age be to try and meet a man through a dating service? When she isn't happy with the results, she takes her ill will to a lawyer to act against a company that has been in business for 40 years. Preposterous. I must have been a little crazy. Why couldn't I go to a bar or a square dance or the library like other women my age? I have no idea.

My daughter received a flyer that said this dating service was looking for seniors who wanted to meet seniors of the opposite sex. Rachel suggested that a year is long enough to be in mourning. She said I might want to phone their office, which was close by, in Glastonbury. After a little cajoling, I acquiesced and gave them a call.

The company was called Love, and with a name like that I should have been suspicious. But I was intrigued. My grown child thought it would be good for me to try and meet an eligible man with interests like mine, one who is breathing, is able to drive at night, and who doesn't have a walker. It was something to consider. The company is in New York with satellite offices all over the East coast and the office I called in Glastonbury is 20 minutes from my house. What did I have to lose? I made a phone call. Priscilla, the aggressive yet pleasant saleswoman, did not let me hang up without scheduling an appointment. She had quite a sales pitch. I made plans to visit the office the next week.

The following Friday I drove to Glastonbury to visit a small, nicely decorated place in a decent office complex. Priscilla was waiting for me. After some initial small talk about the usual – where I live, the weather, my outgoing personality (which of course she said would be great for dating), and a few more questions like how many children and grandchildren I have – she asked, "Do you mind if we do an interest survey so we will be able to couple you with someone suitable?"

"Sounds good to me," I said. We proceeded to spend an hour going over people skills, attitudes, interests, pet peeves, and ego states. Wow! I felt confident that she captured my essence. Of course she would find someone with my interests and attitudes. The one thing I mentioned was that I didn't care about race, religion, or ethnicity; I just didn't want anyone who was overly religious. She assured me that my match would be found in less than two weeks.

I was interested. She could tell. She must have known that this was the right time to bring out the three cards with an amount written on each of them. I gasped.

"These figures are quite high," I uttered.

"Well, you will be meeting someone wonderful. That has to cost you something." I understood that, however, these four figures all depended on which plan I decided to take. I could have a nice trip for any one of the amounts she showed me. I thought for a moment and said, "I will think about it and let you know."

"We happen to have several nice men in mind for you, a few good matches. If you wait, they might be dating someone else."

"I guess I will have to take that chance. I usually don't spend this kind of money without thinking it over. I also want to talk to my children."

"Look, if you sign up now, we'll throw in three additional introductions. If you sign up for the highest priced plan, we will do a background check on these men, not just the usual criminal investigation." She talked about the available men waiting to meet women and did all but tie me to the chair. I felt trapped. I asked the most important question. "Will all the men be paying one of the three figures that I will be paying?"

"Absolutely." I am sometimes impulsive, but not when it involves that kind of money. I guess I was feeling particularly vulnerable that week. I missed George and thought about how happy he always wanted me to be.

"Where do I sign?" I took the most expensive plan. Sixteen introductions with background research and criminal checks. Priscilla seemed to gauge my personality type so carefully, almost like the Myers-Briggs Type Indicator (MBTI). That test was first created in 1944 and was widely used in the 1970s. It is still administered to millions of people, mostly for job compatibility. It can work for marriage counseling, so why not for dating?

I went home pleased. It took courage to pay nearly $10,000 to meet a man-friend. It was explained to me that they had to check my background. That made sense. I was also told that I would have a counselor in the New York office to speak with at some point. A few days later I got a phone call from the person Priscilla mentioned, from New York, telling me that I would be meeting Lou. This man lived about an hour north of West Hartford. Lou called the following day. We planned to have our encounter at a restaurant in Windsor, 25 minutes from home. He called on Monday and wanted to meet on Friday, but I was leaving for Florida that Friday. We decided on Thursday evening. It was the beginning of March 2013 and a snowstorm was in the forecast for Thursday. It hadn't started to snow yet and it was 6:00 p.m. I drove to the restaurant and Lou arrived at the same time. I recognized him mainly from intuition. He reminded me of a slightly thinner, shorter George. He had the same hairline (no hair on his head, but a beautifully coiffed mustache and beard). We hadn't been in the restaurant for 30 minutes when it started to snow, very hard. We decided to leave after a soft drink and a quick appetizer. I reiterated that I was leaving for Florida the next day. He asked if we could get together when I returned and I said "yes." I wasn't overly impressed, but decided to be fair and give it a chance. We had only conversed for a half hour.

I returned from Florida the following week with a badly sprained ankle. Lou called, and we planned a meeting at the same restaurant. I could barely walk. I hobbled into the restaurant and Lou was waiting. We started to talk about children and grandchildren and he told me that he had been married twice, had one daughter and was not too happy with her. He explained that she was giving up her religion and he went to church every day during Lent, and several days during the week throughout the year. He couldn't bear the fact that she wasn't going to be a Catholic. I was surprised that the service introduced me to a person who was religious, since that was the only requirement I felt strongly about. He said that he had a free three-month trial membership with the dating service. He made it clear that he couldn't afford to join without it. Although I told Priscilla I wanted to meet someone who reads and is interested in all the arts, Lou hadn't read a book since high school. When I mentioned that my granddaughter had been in the play *Les Misérables*, he wanted to know what that was. A reverse mortgage was on his mind, as he might lose his house. I decided it was time to leave. He wanted a therapist and a mortgage broker, not a friend to date. Goodbye Lou.

I called the service the next day and suggested that not only was Lou a poor match for me, but the deal wasn't right for me. I also said they violated the most important principle which was that the men pay an equivalent amount of fees. She brushed that aside and said she wanted to introduce me to a new person. I was still limping around with a sprained ankle, but decided to meet Bob. We had a fun conversation by phone, and decided to meet at a local pub on St. Patrick's Day. I got a ride to the bar and waited half an hour. Just as I was ready to leave, a man showed up with sincere apologies. He wasn't necessarily the king or duke they promised, but he was nice looking. We sat at a booth with a couple we didn't know because it was crowded and I had to sit. Bob was a bit presumptuous. He put his arm around me and acted as if we knew each other for years. It was a noisy bar, and Bob had a few other places to visit. I think he went to a few celebratory places before we met. We left after half an hour, each going our separate ways. He called the next day and asked if we could get together on Saturday. I agreed. He asked what I would like to do and I suggested a quick supper and a comedy club. He said "Great."

We planned on meeting at a restaurant close to my building. I was still in a walking boot. I managed to get to the restaurant with the help of a friend, and waited a half-hour, once again, for Bob to make his entrance. At this point we were going to be late for the comedy club if we were going to eat. He proceeded to order a martini and said he didn't care too much about eating. He was obviously inebriated.

I couldn't carry on a civil conversation. He said, "You don't seem to appreciate my humor," to which I replied, "You are correct." I was anxious to leave. He got that message and said, "Maybe I should just leave." I agreed.

He put 20 dollars on the table and got up to make his exit. I had to hobble home. It was not that far, but the distance put pressure on an already bad ankle. Oh, my. What was I thinking when I joined this service? He also mentioned that he paid a modest amount of money to join, nothing even close to what I was paying.

Bob called about five times to apologize, but I never picked up his call. I called New York and spoke to my counselor, asking for a refund. What kind of men am I meeting? She refused to refund the money and said I had to have patience. Where are all the men I was informed about with interests like mine? A religious fanatic and a drunk!

About three weeks passed before I got a call from New York telling me about a very special guy from the Connecticut shore who was a journalist. Hmm, things were looking up. Paul called the next day and we made plans to meet halfway. Yes, he worked for a newspaper for many years... as a machinist. Journalist, no way. He didn't read because of a learning disability. He had never been to a play, only travelled with the Navy, and was looking for the mother who left him when he was three. Get me out of here.

I called the service the next day and asked about their background research. I said, "This is ridiculous, and I want a refund, partial will be fine." My counselor said "No, sorry, you have to be patient." She also mentioned that most men my age want a woman 20 years younger.

"Why didn't they tell me that when I joined?" I asked. The next day I called a lawyer and put the matter in her hands. I saw my lawyer's husband at a gathering recently and he said, "You are making my wife famous." She was quite talented and won the case, and I believe she distinguished herself. I think the experience taught us both something about how dating services can take advantage of innocent women.

24

Changed Expectations

Therapists like me think and write about the components that link people together. I have done counseling and writing about what makes two people happy or unhappy for the last 37 years. Hundreds of couples struggling with marital issues have come to me for guidance. When two people are no longer able to share thoughts and feelings, the relationship starts to break down. Much of the information I've gathered came from textbooks, seminars, and people with whom I have worked. I had never examined relationships from first-hand involvement until now.

My husband Allan, the father of my children, was a master of finding humor in every situation. We created a pair of imaginary animals, one Beagle we called Stogy, named after my father's cigar, and Rufus, a Golden Retriever who reminded us of the cowardly lion in *The Wizard of Oz*. Until we had children, these pets took the blame for everything that went wrong in our household, including clothes left on the floor or dishes in the sink. When Allan had his first heart attack at 42, his ailment put a strain on our marriage. I was afraid to distress him and kept many issues to myself. I might have created some distance, but we were still harmonious and rarely argued. We were happy and grateful for what we had, the gift of a privileged life and two wonderful daughters.

I never thought about our relationship, I just loved.

George was emotionally more autonomous than Allan but wanted to participate in most activities with me. Even during his busy times, George would choose to drive and wait in the car while I did errands. He was pleased to do a crossword puzzle or read a book. I gave up some of my independence, but the companionship worked well.

I was fortunate. I had a loving marriage and a caring 12-year live-in partnership. Both relationships ended with my partner's death. After a period of bereavement and reflection, I dated several people. I unexpectedly met a man who warmed my heart. I assumed I would never meet anyone comparable to Allan or George. I thought I had when I met Joe.

In my work, I learned that chemistry, good understanding, and rapport attract people at the beginning, and decent communication keeps them captivated. Joe and I had a mutual attraction. He said that I was his miracle, and he cared for me deeply. I looked forward to being with him. He sent me emails every morning and throughout the day. We enjoyed plays, museums, and movies. We visited my family. He enjoyed them, and they became his loved ones as well. Two of his three daughters didn't speak to him, and he didn't know why. His parents didn't have any connection with him before they died, and he was estranged from his brother and sister. He wasn't on good terms with his two previous wives. Unfortunate man! He was a victim.

We were spontaneous. Life seemed exciting. Unfortunately, three months after we met, Joe found out he had a serious health problem. Concerned about his well-being and living alone, he started staying at my place. Living together at this stage of our relationship wasn't appropriate; it was too soon. He never moved out. He eventually gave up his apartment and became my "roommate." He had chronic back pain and needed several naps each day over a weekend, so daytime excursions were nonexistent. Our outdoor walks consisted of finding his car in a crowded parking lot. He preferred watching movies in my condo, mostly old mysteries. Theater wasn't important to him anymore as the seats hurt his back. I resumed my tradition of going to spectator events with my female friends.

At some point, less than a year later, I realized that we had different communication styles and they weren't well-matched. If I disagreed with him, he became quiet and pouted. When I initiated a conversation about a problem between us, Joe grew silent at first but ultimately became angry. He was bright, opinionated, and knew what was right for everyone but himself. Joe remembered everything, and what went awry was always my fault. He never hesitated to share that with me.

My major complaint about my experience was the change in Joe's attitude, which started out as magnetism and developed into antagonism. I felt as if I was a supporting actor in a low-ranking horror film. When his infatuation wore off, I discovered that Joe was betraying me, lying, and planning to leave without telling me. The truth was foreign to Joe, and he'd get furious if I pointed it out to him. Why was I unable to tell him to move out? I wanted this connection to be flawless, so I ignored all the red flags that were obvious. He was nothing that he appeared to be. I went into mourning when he left. I realized how deceived I had been. As a psychologist, how could I have been fooled by all his separations, and not have any understanding of the significance? This man was incapable of experiencing anything deep and lasting. If he stayed with someone longer than with me, it was because of children or finances. It didn't matter who I was. He didn't see me. I was another woman with whom he got bored. If I didn't agree with his viewpoint, I didn't count.

I cannot say why, but we became friends after the breakup. We saw each other weekly. No romance, but we were superficially acquainted. We didn't have anyone else romantically in our lives, so we "hung out." It wasn't a good idea, as it kept me from seeing other men in my life as possible companions.

I started to look at relationships differently, including mine. Resolving issues with another person is not always possible. It is hard to delve into submerged feelings if the other person is hostile and disrespectful.

These underlying feelings of anger and contempt can form for years. If the person doesn't care to solve the problem, but instead withdraws or makes the other person feel flawed, there isn't much hope for the connection. Conversations begin poorly and end the same way. There is a difference between having a concern with what your partner is doing, and a personal reproach which can also mean, "You have the problem, I have no part." If there aren't children or finances to keep the couple together, it will often end.

I find it amazing that two people can continue to stay content with different personalities and decidedly dissimilar temperaments. When a partner is discouraged, disheartened, and angry, it is difficult to find pleasure without help. All partners have their arguments. How a couple handles its conflicts might be an indication as to whether the relationship will last. If two people do not learn amicable ways to settle their gripes, the twosome will not flourish.

I know Joe and I would have never found harmonious ways to settle our differences. He was regularly in a blame mode, and always right. Could I continuously be wrong? It felt that way. It became hard work. My relationships with Allan and George, although not perfect, were effortless.

Is there a secret to a successful relationship? Perhaps it has more to do with friendship and open communication than passion or common interests. Thirty-seven years of work as a psychologist and couple's counselor, two intense associations, and several lesser relationships have taught me that what is essential to a happy connection between folks, along with love, is sincerity, hope, and trust.

I have come full circle. I started my life in an apartment building, and although this unit is more luxurious than the one I lived in growing up, it is still an apartment building. I have neighbors within proximity to my place, the way I had in The Bronx. This complex is in the middle of the city, and being here is as close to living in the Big Apple as I will ever be, or as near as I would want to be. I have all the advantages of an urban area right here in West Hartford. Unlike New York, it is quiet after midnight when I finally go to sleep. I live alone, once again, with no desire to find a live-in partner, unless I become in need of someone to care for my well-being.

My place is walking distance to the movies, a hair salon, shops, and restaurants, where many of the managers know me, and where I can get a reservation for dinner on short notice. I see people going places and doing things, and I can view this life through three "curtain less" windows from a corner of this condominium compound. I can watch the sun rise slowly behind the trees spreading through the sky. I can hear the wind beat upon the land, and I can feel the rain drop to the earth below…without getting wet.

I will always miss the joyous moments I shared with George at our house opposite the reservoir in West Hartford. We played music in the morning while we read the paper or completed a crossword puzzle. Our coffee brewed in an old-fashioned pot. We often discussed what we might have for dinner and who would shop for it. There was a quiet calmness, a comfort. Both Allan and George were the right partners, people to love and to share my life.

Material things stopped mattering to me even before I moved here. I donated sets of dishes, kitchen gear, tables, and clothing to others. My extra closet is almost empty, and so are many drawers. I don't need or want more things. There is a freedom I feel with less possessions that can be described as letting go. I'm not a philosopher, but I am interested in transformation, understanding, and healing. I want more joy in my life, to be more gratified, fulfilled and real. For me, this means getting rid of accessories and emotions that are distractions – not only things, but long conversations about topics I don't need to know details about, too much web surfing, eating poorly, things that don't add to my goal of creating what I want. These thoughts will probably take me the rest of my life to put into action, but I am in no hurry. In the meantime, I have many friends to enjoy, if I choose to be with them, including a new man I am dating. I spend quality time by myself. There are advantages to living alone. I can go wherever I want and stay if I wish. I can spend a weekend reading, writing, and watching movies, if that is my desire. I don't have to make conversation with anyone and I don't have to answer the phone. The house stays as neat as I keep it.

Those who are close to me have noticed that I'm more genuine, more compassionate, and more confident as I get closer to the finish line. I learned to accept life as it evolves; I'm not passive, I stay busy, affirm my needs and interests, and find calm within the storm. I am more balanced. I still question most things, and I'm open to unforeseen answers. As Einstein said, "I am surprised by nothing at all or by everything that is."

25

...And Now

There is no sidestepping trouble in our lives. In April 2018, a few months after my 80th birthday, I received some surprising news. I had a growing nodule on my back and a smaller, but similar lump on my left thigh. I pointed these irregularities out to my dermatologist, and she said they were "nothing." I felt a new lump under the skin on my back, next to the one that looked like a large cyst, five months after the first two. I thought it was time to see my oncologist. She suggested a biopsy. A few weeks later the surgeon called me with my diagnoses of Lymphoma.

How could I have a disease, and a highly aggressive form of it, according to my new oncologist, be so sick, and feel fine? I still worked and saw a half dozen clients each week. I rented an office in the medical building next door after the homeowner's association in my condominium complex insisted I no longer see people in my home. I visited with friends and family on a regular basis and went to see the series of plays I subscribed to each season. Writing was important to me and I attended a new class with a dazzling instructor who became my friend. I traveled to Ireland with my daughter, Rachel, and a few months before I was diagnosed, the two of us went to Florida.

I was referred to a new oncologist/ hematologist at Saint Francis Hospital who specialized in my disease, and soon after, I went to Yale, New Haven to consult with another professional in the field of blood disorders. The doctor at Yale reinforced my surprise that these lesions weren't recognized by my dermatologist. My local oncologist said my lymphoma was cutaneous, skin type, and often hard to recognize. He said she is a fine physician, and mistakes happen. I would've had lymphoma, whether or not it was known earlier. I might not have had it as aggressively if it were diagnosed earlier. I wrote the dermatologist a letter; she immediately called. We had several discussions. She wasn't defensive, and apologized for not following my concern. I decided to continue with her, and I am glad that I did. She was my doctor for many years and I was satisfied.

There were several treatment options to consider, but my oncologist, a wise and caring man, said we should "go for broke." This meant rejecting the outpatient chemotherapy treatment every three weeks, which was less invasive, and pondering the five-day hospital stay every 21 days for six treatments. That lasted about four months. My blood counts decreased, which meant a lower immune system.

I grew highly susceptible to germs and diseases. My life became different. No movies, theater, restaurants, or other people's homes, even my daughter's. They had dogs, children staying with them at different times with friends, and the commotion that goes along with a family. I avoided eating many foods I enjoyed that could be a problem because of bacteria: raw vegetables, salads, and uncooked fish like sashimi, my way of getting Omega 3 in my diet. I also avoided certain vegetables like broccoli and cauliflower, and all berries and fruit that I couldn't peel. These foods were missed, but four months wasn't that long.

I sadly missed my granddaughter Zoe's graduation from Trinity College. I was going to officiate at Yuko and her fiancé Dave's wedding. I was a Universalist Minister and looking forward to that occasion for months, but wasn't able to solemnize their wedding, nor could I attend.

I called this time, "my house arrest."

My oncologist didn't want me to be alone. Many complications could arise. I hired Mary to assist me with household chores, cook at night if I was tired, and drive, a precaution in case I wasn't feeling well enough to have my blood checked each week at the hospital or if I was sick from the chemotherapy. I was fortunate. Everything was bearable. I never felt overly ill or exceedingly tired. I cooked with Mary's help and drove with no problem.

Mary was from Ghana, living in Pennsylvania, and working for an agency in Connecticut. We became good friends during the four months that she stayed with me.

She was an astute woman who knew how to be scarce when I wanted alone time, and after a few heart-to-heart chats, she developed better communication skills about her needs.

Life is all about timing. No one put it better than King Solomon in The Bible. Ecclesiastes 3, "there is an appointed time for everything. And there is a time for every event under heaven – A time to give birth, and a time to die…" This was my time to be ill. For the first time, I stayed home meditating, reading, watching television, and seeing friends and family. I had high hopes for remission or recovery. My time to enter the hospital went by faster than the hospital stays. The nurses and staff were warm, intelligent and available when required. I felt well and disliked being a patient. I made sure to bathe without the use of a tub or shower each morning and to dress in my street clothes. I wasn't going to feel like an inmate. I had a pole with the chemo drugs attached to me, and together we walked the halls each morning. I calculated that 525 walks up and down the hall would equal a mile. I never got past 50, but it was something to contemplate. I named my pole Athena, the Greek goddess of wisdom and war. I imagined that between us, we had the courage required to deal with what was in store for me, and the inspiration to get better. This was my war, and with her help, (the chemo) I expected to be victorious.

William Shakespeare wrote about the effects of time in many of his sonnets and plays. One of the best known is in Macbeth, "Tomorrow and tomorrow and tomorrow, Creeps in this petty pace from day to day." Henry Van

Dyke wrote about the passage of time and our relationship to it. "Time is too slow for those who wait, and it was."

It was Spring, then Summer and I became a television addict. I got hooked on Turkish and Spanish soap operas, shows with 60 or so episodes. They held my attention. They all had subtitles, so the only time I turned off the TV was to eat, or I would miss something. I downloaded many episodes to my iPad for my hospital stays and watched them with passion. They took my mind off myself and my surroundings. At home it was different. I didn't mind the silence and serenity.

Alexander Pope wrote about how time steals our youth and our very lives. "Years following years steal something ev'ry day. At last they steal us from ourselves away." I fantasized about my formative years and how I was physically more able to cope with this disease. I no longer cared that much about doing things, I just wanted to be well. I enjoyed life as it was, from moment to moment. I didn't have a "bucket" list.

Time dictates so much of our lives and experiences and we are bound to respect its passage, regardless of whether we wish to or not.

I had flashes of being grateful, as I felt well, and had boundless support.

I don't have enough words to describe the love I feel for my children. They were helpful and considerate. They shopped for me, accompanied me to various doctor appointments, visited at home and in the hospital. They gave me undivided attention. "A moment in my tummy, a lifetime in my heart." I received phone calls from my daughters more than once a day. My sons-in-laws were like sons; they called and visited without their wives. I felt a love for all of them that was full of joy. They made me happy and proud.

My grandchildren called daily. Emily and Zoe live in New York, but it was as if they lived in town. Meg was in California for the summer, and with the three-hour time difference, we spoke weekly. They were beautiful and solid. Along with my children, they are the finest things in my life. They were, and continue to be, amazing.

So many good friends, at the hospital and at home, washing their hands upon arriving and wearing masks when required. I cannot imagine my life without them.

Albert Einstein quotes, "The only reason for time is so that everything doesn't happen at once." Blood tests, injections to bring up the blood counts, doctors' appointments, outpatient chemo, in hospital chemo. I was busy, and usually optimistic and well-maintained.

I finished my chemotherapy at the end of August and started three weeks of radiation. On October 31, 2018, I finished the prescribed regiment.

My routine started again: visiting friends and family, writing, dining out, and consulting with patients over the phone. Owen Meredith muses: "However we pass Time, he passes still, Passing away whatever the pastime, And whether we use him well or ill, some day he gives us the slip for the last time."

Appreciatively, it wasn't my time.

During my illness, I became more spiritual. I have

never been religious, but I now had faith. I was aware of a higher power. I wasn't sure what form it took, but its presence was there for me to reflect upon. I was peaceful. I developed greater acceptance of other people, their kindnesses, concerns and limitations. Each person copes with life differently and is unique and valuable, and they all have a special place in my heart.

In January 2019, I noticed a blemish on my stomach. I thought it was prudent for me to call my oncologist. He thought a biopsy was necessary, which eventually showed that I did relapse, but it was localized in that one place. I followed it with a PET scan that showed no other disease in my body. I also paid a visit to the other oncologist at Yale. My oncologist at Saint Francis said he had to use his imagination to find the mark.

Back to radiation for two weeks, and then some prescribed medication, indefinitely. I was disappointed, but still hoped that recovery or remission was possible.

A wise friend told me, "You can't change the past, but you can ruin the present by worrying about the future."

About Bernice Schaefer

Bernice Schaefer is a psychologist and marriage and family therapist in West Hartford, Connecticut. Born in New York City, she spent many years acting, directing, and eventually teaching. In addition to her involvement in all aspects of the theater, she became a Certified Psychodramatist, an individual psychotherapy that is accomplished within a group. It engages guided dramatic action to explore problems. Bernice eventually received a Ph.D. in Psychology and has been in private practice for the last 37 years.

www.ingramcontent.com/pod-product-compliance
Lightning Source LLC
Chambersburg PA
CBHW060521130626
46553CB00002B/599